An ILO code of practice

Safety and health in construction

International Labour Office   Geneva

ILO
Safety and health in construction: An ILO code of practice
Geneva, International Labour Office, 1992

/Code of practice/, /Occupational safety/, /Occupational health/, /Construction industry/. 08.10.1
ISBN 92-2-107104-9

Also published in French: *Sécurité et santé dans la construction*. Recueil de directives pratiques du BIT (ISBN 92-2-207104-2), Geneva, 1992; and in Spanish: *Seguridad y salud en la construcción*. Repertorio de recomendaciones prácticas de la OIT (ISBN 92-2-307104-6), Geneva, 1992

ILO Cataloguing in Publication Data

Printed in Switzerland   ATA

Preface

In accordance with the decision taken by the Governing Body of the ILO at its 244th Session (November 1989), a meeting of experts was convened in Geneva from 12 to 19 March 1991 to draw up a code of practice on safety and health in construction. The meeting was composed of 21 experts, seven appointed following consultations with governments, seven following consultations with the Employers' group and seven following consultations with the Workers' group of the Governing Body.[1] After examining and finalising

---

[1] *Experts appointed following consultations with governments:*

Mr. J.-P. Clément, Ministry of Labour, Employment and Vocational Training, Paris (France).

Mr. D. G. Kibara, Ministry of Labour, Nairobi (Kenya).

Mr. W. Kukulski, Institute for Building Technology, Warsaw (Poland).

Mr. S. S. Msangi, Ministry of Labour and Youth Development, Dar es Salaam (United Republic of Tanzania).

Ms. M. H. Negrão, Ministry of Labour and Social Welfare, São Paulo (Brazil).

Mr. A. Sanchez, Director, Department of Labour and Employment, Manila (Philippines).

Mr. H. Wong Kok Choy, Ministry of Labour, Singapore (Singapore).

Experts appointed following consultations with the Employers' group:

Mr. J. A. DeVries, Canadian Construction Association, Ottawa, Ontario (Canada).

Mr. H. Georget, National Union for Small and Medium Industrial Enterprises in the Niger (SYNAPEMEIN), Niamey (Niger).

Mr. W. M. Nasr, Fana Investment and Trading Inc., Beirut (Lebanon).

Dr. E. J. Ríos Márquez, Uruguayan Construction League, Montevideo (Uruguay).

Mr. J. Skau-Jacobsen, Associated General Contractors of Norway, Oslo (Norway), replaced in the second part of the meeting by Mr. G. Berglund, Swedish Construction Federation, Stockholm (Sweden).

(footnote continued overleaf)

the text, based on a draft prepared by the Office, the experts adopted this code.

The practical recommendations of this code of practice are intended for the use of all those, both in public and the private sectors, who have responsibility for safety and health in construction. The code is not intended to replace national laws or regulations or accepted standards. It has been drawn up with the object of providing guidance to those who may be engaged in the framing of provisions of this kind; in particular, governmental or other public authorities, committees, management or employers' and workers' organisations in this industrial sector.

Mr. P. M. Walsh, National Authority for Health and Safety, G T Crampton Ltd., Dublin (Ireland).

Mr. Wan Hock Leong, Sato Kogyo Co. Ltd., Kuala Lumpur (Malaysia).

Experts appointed following consultations with the Workers' group:

Mr. T. Escorial Clemente, State Federation for Wood, Construction and Related Industries (FEMCAUGT), Madrid (Spain).

Mr. B. Laguna, Workers' Federation for the Construction Industry in Venezuela (FETRACONSTRUCCION), Caracas (Venezuela).

Mr. J. Martins, Union for Technicians and Employees in Civil Engineering, Public Works and Related Industries (SETACOOP), Lisbon (Portugal).

Mr. A. Russ, New Zealand Building Trades Union, Wellington (New Zealand).

Mr. M. F. Sissoko, National Workers' Union of Mali (UNTM), Bamako (Mali).

Mr. N. Tobiassen, Trade Safety Council Workers' Secretariat, Copenhagen (Denmark).

Mr. A. Zverev, Building Workers' Federation, c/o General Confederation of Soviet Trade Unions, Moscow (USSR).

International governmental and non-governmental organisations represented:

World Health Organization.

Commission of European Communities.

International Organization for Standardization.

Local circumstances and technical possibilities will determine how far it is practicable to follow its provisions. Furthermore, these provisions should be read in the context of conditions in the country proposing to use this information, the scale of operation involved and technical facilities.

The text of the code was approved for publication by the Governing Body of the ILO at its 250th Session (May-June 1991).

International Social Security Association.

International Organisation of Employers.

International Confederation of Free Trade Unions.

World Confederation of Labour.

World Federation of Trade Unions.

International Federation of Building and Woodworkers.

Trade Unions International of Workers in the Building, Wood and Building Materials Industry.

ILO representatives:

Dr. K. Kogi, Chief, Occupational Safety and Health Branch.

Dr. J. Serbitzer, Safety Engineer, Occupational Safety and Health Branch.

ILO consultants:

Mr. K. C. Gupta, Director-General, Directorate General, Factory Advice Service and Labour Institutes, Bombay (India).

Mr. J. Hinksman, Regional Director of Field Operations, Health and Safety Executive, London (United Kingdom).

Contents

1. General provisions

1.1. Objective

1.1.1. The objective of this code is to provide practical guidance on a legal, administrative, technical and educational framework for safety and health in construction with a view to:

(a) preventing accidents and diseases and harmful effects on the health of workers arising from employment in construction;

(b) ensuring appropriate design and implementation of construction projects;

(c) providing means of analysing from the point of view of safety, health and working conditions, construction processes, activities, technologies and operations, and of taking appropriate measures of planning, control and enforcement.

1.1.2. This code also provides guidance in the implementation of the provisions of the Safety and Health in Construction Convention, 1988 (No. 167), and the Safety and Health in Construction Recommendation, 1988 (No. 175).

1.2. Application

1.2.1. This code applies to:

(a) construction activities which cover:

  (i) building, including excavation and the construction, structural alteration, renovation, repair, maintenance (including cleaning and painting) and demolition of all types of buildings or structures;

  (ii) civil engineering, including excavation and the construction, structural alteration, repair, maintenance and demolition of, for example, airports, docks, harbours, inland waterways, dams, river and avalanche and sea defence works, roads and highways, railways, bridges, tunnels, viaducts and works related to the provision of services such as communications, drainage, sewerage, water and energy supplies;

(iii) the erection and dismantling of prefabricated buildings and structures, as well as the manufacturing of prefabricated elements on the construction site;

(b) the fabrication and erection of oil rigs and of offshore installations while under construction on shore.

1.2.2.   The provisions of this code should be considered as the basic requirements for protecting workers' safety and health.

1.2.3.   The provisions of this code should be applied to self-employed persons as may be specified by national laws or regulations.

1.3. Definitions

In this code, the following terms have the meanings hereby assigned to them:

Adequate, appropriate or suitable are used to describe qualitatively or quantitatively the means or method used to protect the worker.

Bearer: see *putlog.*

Brace: A structural member that holds one point in a fixed position with respect to another point; bracing is a system of structural members designed to prevent distortion of a structure.

By hand: The work is done without the help of a mechanised tool.

Cartridge-operated: A device in which an explosive drives a projectile such as a nail or a stud into materials; they are of three types:

(i) "*high-velocity type*", in which the projectile is driven directly by the gases from the explosive charge;

(ii) "*low-velocity piston type*", in which the gases from the explosive charge drive a piston which propels the projectile;

(iii) "*hammer-operated low-velocity piston type*", in which the piston is driven by a hammer blow in addition to the gases from the explosive charge.

Client: Any natural or legal person for whom a project is carried out.

Code of practice: A document offering practical guidance on the policy and standard setting in occupational safety and health for use by governments, employers, workers and any other persons involved in the construction process in order to promote safety and health at the national level and at the level of the enterprise.

Competent authority: A minister, government department, or other public authority having the power to issue regulations, orders or other instructions having the force of law.

Competent person: A person possessing adequate qualifications, such as suitable training and sufficient knowledge, experience and skill for the safe performance of the specific work. The competent authorities may define appropriate criteria for the designation of such persons and may determine the duties to be assigned to them.

Construction: Those activities as defined in paragraph 1.2.1.

Construction site: Any site at which any of the processes or operations described in paragraph 1.2.1. are carried on.

Danger: Danger of accident or injury to health.

Employer:

(i) Any physical or legal person who employs one or more workers on a construction site; and

(ii) as the context requires, the principal contractor, the contractor or the subcontractor.

3

Guard-rail: An adequately secured rail erected along an exposed edge to prevent persons from falling.

Hazard: Danger or potential danger.

Hoist: A machine which lifts materials or persons by means of a platform which runs on guides.

Ledger: A scaffold member which extends longitudinally and horizontally parallel to the face of a structure, at right angles to the putlogs and which supports the putlogs, forms a tie between the posts, and becomes a part of the scaffold bracing; ledgers which do not support putlogs are also called stringers.

Lifting appliance: Any stationary or mobile appliance used for raising or lowering persons or loads.

Lifting gear: Any gear or tackle by means of which a load can be attached to a lifting appliance but which does not form an integral part of the appliance or load.

Means of access or egress: Passageways, corridors, stairs, platforms, ladders and any other means to be used by persons for normally entering or leaving the workplace or for escaping in case of danger.

Putlog or *bearer:* A scaffold member upon which the platform rests. In a single pole scaffold the outer end of the putlog rests on a ledger and the inner end rests in the wall; in an independent pole scaffold each end of the putlog rests on a ledger; in an independent pole scaffold a putlog is known as a bearer.

Raker: An inclined load-bearing tube or pole.

Safety extra-low voltage: A nominal voltage not exceeding 42 V between conductors, or, in the case of phase circuits, not exceeding 24 V between conductors and neutral, the no-load voltage of the circuit not exceeding 50 V and 29 V respectively.

Scaffold: Any temporary structure, fixed, suspended or mobile, and its supporting components which is used for supporting workers and materials or to gain access to any such structure, and which is not a "lifting appliance" as defined above.

Sound or good construction: Construction conforming to any relevant standards issued by a national standardising institution or other body recognised by the competent authority, or to generally accepted international engineering practices or other technical standards.

Sound or good material: Material of a quality conforming to any relevant standards issued by a national standardising institution or other body recognised by the competent authority or to generally accepted international engineering practices or other technical standards.

Standard (upright or post)*:* In relation to a scaffold, a vertical or near vertical tube which bears the weight of a scaffold and its load and includes a through tie or a reveal tie or a bore tie; a through tie is a tie assembly through a window or other opening in a wall; a reveal tie is an assembly of a reveal tube with wedges or screwed fittings or pads fixed between the opposing faces of an opening in a wall together with the tie tube.

Toe-board: A barrier placed along the edge of a scaffold platform, runway, etc., and secured there to guard against the slipping of persons or the falling of material.

Transom: A tube spanning across ledger to form the support for boards forming the working platform or to connect the outer standards to the inner standards.

Worker: Any person engaged in construction.

Workplace: All places where workers need to be or to go by reason of their work and which are under the control of an employer as defined in "employer".

2. General duties

2.1. General duties of competent authorities

2.1.1. The competent authorities should, on the basis of an assessment of the safety and health hazards involved and in consultation with the most representative organisation of employers and workers, adopt and maintain in force national laws or regulations to ensure the safety and health of workers employed in construction projects and to protect persons at, or in the vicinity of, a construction site from all risks which may arise from such site.

2.1.2. The national laws and regulations adopted in pursuance of paragraph 2.1.1 above should provide for their practical application through technical standards or codes of practice, or by other appropriate methods consistent with national conditions and practices.

2.1.3. In giving effect to paragraphs 2.1.1 and 2.1.2 above, each competent authority should have due regard to the relevant standards adopted by recognised international organisations in the field of standardisation.

2.1.4. The competent authority should provide appropriate inspection services to enforce or administer the application of the provisions of the national laws and regulations and provide these services with the resources necessary for the accomplishment of their task, or satisfy itself that appropriate inspection is carried out.

2.1.5. The measures to be taken to ensure that there is organised co-operation between employers and workers to promote safety and health at construction sites should be prescribed by national laws or regulations or by the competent authority. Such measures should include:

(a) the establishment of safety and health committees representative of employers and workers with such powers and duties as may be prescribed;

(b) the election or appointment of workers' safety delegates with such powers and duties as may be prescribed;

(c) the appointment by the employer of suitably qualified and experienced persons to promote safety and health;

(d) the training of safety delegates and safety and health committee members.

2.1.6. National laws or regulations should provide for the notification by the client to the competent authority of construction sites of such size, duration or characteristics in accordance with such time schedule as may be prescribed.

2.1.7. National laws or regulations should provide for general duties of clients, designers, engineers and architects to take into consideration the safety and health aspects in the designing of buildings, structures or construction projects.

2.2. General duties of employers

2.2.1. Employers should provide adequate means and organisation and should establish a suitable programme on the safety and health of workers consistent with national laws and regulations and should comply with the prescribed safety and health measures at the workplace.

2.2.2. Employers should so provide and maintain workplaces, plant, equipment, tools and machinery and so organise construction work that as far as is reasonably practicable there is no risk of accident or injury to health of workers. In particular, construction work should be so planned, prepared and undertaken that:

(a) dangers liable to arise at the workplace are prevented as soon as possible;

(b) excessively or unnecessarily strenuous work positions and movements are avoided;

(c) organisation of work takes into account the safety and health of workers;

(d) materials and products are used which are suitable from a safety and health point of view;

(e) working methods are employed which protect workers against the harmful effects of chemical, physical and biological agents.

2.2.3.   Employers should establish committees with representatives of workers and management or make other suitable arrangement consistent with national laws and regulations for the participation of workers in ensuring safe working conditions.

2.2.4.   Employers should take all appropriate precautions to protect persons present at, or in the vicinity of, a construction site from all risks which may arise from such site.

2.2.5.   Employers should arrange for regular safety inspections by competent persons at suitable intervals of all buildings, plant, equipment, tools, machinery, workplaces and systems of work under the control of the employer at construction sites in accordance with national laws, regulations, standards or codes of practice. As appropriate, the competent person should examine and test by type or individually to ascertain the safety of construction machinery and equipment.

2.2.6.   When acquiring plant, equipment or machinery, employers should ensure that it takes account of ergonomic principles in its design and conforms to relevant national laws, regulations, standards or codes of practice and, if there are none, that it is so designed or protected that it can be operated safely and without risk to health.

2.2.7.   Employers should provide such supervision as will ensure that workers perform their work with due regard to their safety and health.

2.2.8. Employers should assign workers only to employment for which they are suited by their age, physique, state of health and skill.

2.2.9. Employers should satisfy themselves that all workers are suitably instructed in the hazards connected with their work and environment and trained in the precautions necessary to avoid accidents and injury to health.

2.2.10. Employers should take all practicable steps to ensure that workers are made aware of the relevant national or local laws, regulations, standards, codes of practice, instructions and advice relating to prevention of accidents and injuries to health.

2.2.11. Buildings, plant, equipment, tools, machinery or workplaces in which a dangerous defect has been found should not be used until the defect has been remedied.

2.2.12. Where there is an imminent danger to the safety of workers, the employer should take immediate steps to stop the operation and evacuate workers as appropriate.

2.2.13. On dispersed sites and where small groups of workers operate in isolation, employers should establish a checking system by which it can be ascertained that all the members of a shift, including operators of mobile equipment, have returned to the camp or base at the close of work.

2.2.14. Employers should provide appropriate first aid, training and welfare facilities to workers and, whenever collective measures are not feasible or are insufficient, provide and maintain personal protective equipment and clothing. Employers should also ensure access for workers to occupational health services.

2.3. General duties of self-employed persons

2.3.1 Self-employed persons should comply with the prescribed safety and health measures at the workplace according to national laws or regulations.

2.4. Co-operation and co-ordination

2.4.1. Whenever two or more employers undertake activities at one construction site, they should co-operate with one another as well as with the client or client's representative and with other persons participating in the construction work being undertaken in the application of the prescribed safety and health measures.

2.4.2. Whenever two or more employers undertake activities simultaneously or successively at one construction site, the principal contractor, or other person or body with actual control over or primary responsibility for overall construction site activities, should be responsible for planning and co-ordinating safety and health measures and, in so far as is compatible with national laws and regulations, for ensuring compliance with such measures.

2.4.3. In so far as is compatible with national laws and regulations, where the principal contractor, or other person or body with actual control over or primary responsibility for overall construction site activities, is not present at the site, they should nominate a competent person or body at the site with the authority and means necessary to ensure on their behalf co-ordination and compliance with safety and health measures.

2.4.4. Employers should remain responsible for the application of the safety and health measures in respect of the workers placed under their authority.

2.4.5. Employers and self-employed persons undertaking

activities simultaneously at a construction site should co-operate fully in the application of safety and health measures.

2.4.6. Employers and designers should liaise effectively on factors affecting safety and health.

2.5. General rights and duties of workers

2.5.1. Workers should have the right and the duty at any workplace to participate in ensuring safe working conditions to the extent of their control over the equipment and methods of work and to express views on working procedures adopted as they may affect safety and health.

2.5.2. Workers should have the right to obtain proper information from the employer regarding safety and health risks and safety and health measures related to the work processes. This information should be presented in forms and languages which the workers easily understand.

2.5.3. Workers should have the right to remove themselves from danger when they have good reason to believe that there is an imminent and serious danger to their safety or health. They should have the duty so to inform their supervisor immediately.

2.5.4. In accordance with national legislation, workers should:

(a) co-operate as closely as possible with their employer in the application of the prescribed safety and health measures;

(b) take reasonable care for their own safety and health and that of other persons who may be affected by their acts or omissions at work;

(c) use and take care of personal protective equipment, protective clothing and facilities placed at their disposal and not misuse anything provided for their own protection or the protection of others;

(d) report forthwith to their immediate supervisor, and to the workers' safety representative where one exists, any situation which they believe could present a risk and which they cannot properly deal with themselves;

(e) comply with the prescribed safety and health measures;

(f) participate in regular safety and health meetings.

2.5.5. Except in an emergency, workers, unless duly authorised, should not interfere with, remove, alter or displace any safety device or other appliance furnished for their protection or the protection of others, or interfere with any method or process adopted with a view to avoiding accidents and injury to health.

2.5.6. Workers should not operate or interfere with plant and equipment that they have not been duly authorised to operate, maintain or use.

2.5.7. Workers should not sleep or rest in dangerous places such as scaffolds, railway tracks, garages, or in the vicinity of fires, dangerous or toxic substances, running machines or vehicles and heavy equipment.

2.6. General duties of designers, engineers, architects

2.6.1. Those concerned with the design and planning of a construction project should receive training in safety and health and should integrate the safety and health of the construction workers into the design and planning process in accordance with national laws, regulations and practice.

2.6.2. Care should be exercised by engineers, architects and other professional persons, not to include anything in the design which would necessitate the use of dangerous structural or other procedures or materials hazardous to health or safety which could be avoided by design modifications or by substitute materials.

2.6.3. Those designing buildings, structures or other construction projects should take into account the safety problems associated with subsequent maintenance and upkeep where maintenance and upkeep would involve special hazards.

2.6.4. Facilities should be included in the design for such work to be performed with the minimum risk.

2.7 General duties of clients

2.7.1 Clients should:

(a) co-ordinate or nominate a competent person to co-ordinate all activities relating to safety and health on their construction projects;

(b) inform all contractors on the project of special risks to health and safety of which the clients are or should be aware;

(c) require those submitting tenders to make provision for the cost of safety and health measures during the construction process.

2.7.2. In estimating the periods for completion of work stages and overall completion of the project, clients should take account of safety and health requirements during the construction process.

3. Safety of workplaces

3.1. General provisions

3.1.1. All appropriate precautions should be taken:

(a) to ensure that all workplaces are safe and without risk of injury to the safety and health of workers;

(b) to protect persons present at or in the vicinity of a construction site from all risks which may arise from such site.

3.1.2. All openings and other areas likely to pose danger to workers should be clearly indicated.

3.2. Means of access and egress

3.2.1. Adequate and safe means of access to and egress from all workplaces should be provided, indicated where appropriate and maintained in a safe condition.

3.3. Housekeeping

3.3.1. A suitable housekeeping programme should be established and continuously implemented on each construction site which should include provisions for:

(a) the proper storage of materials and equipment;

(b) the removal of scrap, waste and debris at appropriate intervals.

3.3.2. Loose materials which are not required for use should not be placed or allowed to accumulate on the site so as to obstruct means of access to and egress from workplaces and passageways.

3.3.3. Workplaces and passageways that are slippery owing to ice, snow, oil or other causes should be cleaned up or strewn with sand, sawdust, ash or the like.

3.4. Precautions against the fall of materials and persons, and collapse of structures

3.4.1. Adequate precautions should be taken such as the provision of fencing, look-out men or barriers to protect any person who might be injured by the fall of materials, or tools or equipment being raised or lowered.

3.4.2. Where necessary to prevent danger, guys, stays or supports should be used or other effective precautions should be taken to prevent the collapse of structures or parts of structures that are being erected, maintained, repaired, dismantled or demolished.

3.4.3. All openings through which workers are liable to fall should be kept effectively covered or fenced and indicated in the most appropriate manner.

3.4.4. As far as practicable, guard-rails and toe-boards in accordance with national laws and regulations should be provided to protect workers from falling from elevated work-places. Wherever the guard-rails and toe-boards cannot be provided:

(a) adequate safety nets or safety sheets should be erected and maintained; or

(b) adequate safety harnesses should be provided and used.

3.5. Prevention of unauthorised entry

3.5.1. Construction sites in built-up areas and alongside vehicular and pedestrian traffic routes should be fenced to prevent the entry of unauthorised persons.

3.5.2. Visitors should not be allowed access to construction sites unless accompanied by or authorised by a competent person and provided with the appropriate protective equipment.

3.6. Fire prevention and fire fighting

3.6.1. All appropriate measures should be taken by the employer to:

(a) avoid the risk of fire;

(b) control quickly and efficiently any outbreak of fire;

(c) bring about a quick and safe evacuation of persons.

3.6.2. Sufficient and suitable storage should be provided for flammable liquids, solids and gases.

3.6.3. Secure storage areas should be provided for flammable liquids, solids and gases such as liquefied petroleum gas cylinders, paints and other such materials in order to deter trespassers.

3.6.4. Smoking should be prohibited and "No Smoking" notices be prominently displayed in all places containing readily combustible or flammable materials.

3.6.5. In confined spaces and other places in which flammable gases, vapours or dusts can cause danger:

(a) only suitably protected electrical installations and equipment, including portable lamps, should be used;

(b) there should be no naked flames or similar means of ignition;

(c) there should be notices prohibiting smoking;

(d) oily rags, waste and clothes or other substances liable to spontaneous ignition should be removed without delay to a safe place;

(e) adequate ventilation should be provided.

3.6.6. Combustible materials such as packing materials, sawdust, greasy/oily waste and scrap wood or plastics should not be allowed to accumulate in workplaces but should be kept in closed metal containers in a safe place.

3.6.7. Regular inspections should be made of places where there are fire risks. These include the vicinity of heating appliances, electrical installations and conductors, stores of flammable and combustible materials, hot welding and cutting operations.

3.6.8. Welding, flame cutting and other hot work should only be done on the orders of a competent supervisor after appropriate precautions, as required, are taken to reduce the risk of fire.

3.6.9. Places where workers are employed should, if necessary to prevent the danger of fire, be provided as far as practicable with:

(a) suitable and sufficient fire-extinguishing equipment, which should be easily visible and accessible;

(b) an adequate water supply at ample pressure.

3.6.10. Fire-extinguishing equipment should be properly maintained and inspected at suitable intervals by a competent person. Access to fire-extinguishing equipment such as hydrants, portable extinguishers and connections for hoses should be kept clear at all times.

3.6.11. All supervisors and a sufficient number of workers should be trained in the use of fire-extinguishing equipment, so that adequate trained personnel are readily available during all working periods.

3.6.12. Where necessary to guard against danger, workers should be suitably trained in the action to be taken in the event of fire, including the use of means of escape.

3.6.13. Where appropriate, suitable visual signs should be provided to indicate clearly the direction of escape in case of fire.

3.6.14. Means of escape should be kept clear at all times. Escape routes should be frequently inspected particularly in high structures and where access is restricted, as in tunnel workings.

3.6.15. Sufficient and suitable means to give warning in case of fire should be provided where this is necessary to prevent danger. Such warning should be clearly audible in all parts of the site where persons are liable to work. There should be an effective evacuation plan so that all persons are evacuated speedily without panic and accounted for and all plant and processes shut down.

3.6.16. Notices should be posted at conspicuous places indicating:

(a) the nearest fire alarm;

(b) the telephone number and address of the nearest emergency services.

3.7. Lighting

3.7.1. Where natural lighting is not adequate to ensure safe working conditions, adequate and suitable lighting, including portable lighting where appropriate, should be provided at every workplace and any other place on the construction site where a worker may have to pass.

3.7.2. Artificial lighting should, as far as practicable, not produce glare or disturbing shadows.

3.7.3. Where necessary to prevent danger, lamps should be protected by suitable guards against accidental breakage.

Safety of workplaces

3.7.4. The cables of portable electrical lighting equipment should be of adequate size and characteristics for the power requirements and of adequate mechanical strength to withstand severe conditions in construction operations.

19

4. Scaffolds and ladders

4.1. General provisions

4.1.1. Where work cannot safely be done on or from the ground or from part of a building or other permanent structure, a safe and suitable scaffold should be provided and maintained or other equally safe and suitable provision should be made.

4.1.2. Scaffolds should be provided with safe means of access, such as stairs, ladders or ramps. Ladders should be secured against inadvertent movement.

4.1.3. All scaffolds and ladders should be constructed, erected and used in accordance with national laws and regulations.

4.1.4. Every scaffold should be properly designed, constructed, erected and maintained so as to prevent collapse or accidental displacement when properly used.

4.1.5. Every scaffold and part thereof should be:

(a) designed so as to prevent hazards for workers during erection and dismantling;

(b) designed so that guard rails and other protective devices, platforms, putlogs, rakers, transoms, ladders, stairs or ramps can be easily put together;

(c) of suitable and sound material and of adequate size and strength for the purpose for which it is to be used and maintained in a proper condition.

4.1.6. The competent authority should establish and enforce laws, regulations or standards covering detailed technical provisions for the design, construction, erection, use, maintenance, dismantling and inspection of the different kinds of scaffolds and ladders used in construction work.

4.2. Materials

4.2.1.   Sufficient suitable and sound material should be provided and used in the construction of scaffolds.

4.2.2.   Timber used in the construction of scaffolds should be straight-grained, sound, and free from large knots, dry rot, worm holes and other defects likely to affect its strength.

4.2.3.   No rope which is defective whether through contact with acids or other corrosive substances or otherwise should be used on scaffolds.

4.2.4.   Where necessary, boards and planks used for scaffolds should be protected against splitting.

4.2.5.   Ladders, boards and planks used in scaffolds should not be painted so that any defects are visible.

4.2.6.   Materials used in the construction of scaffolds should be stored under good conditions and apart from any material unsuitable for scaffolds.

4.2.7.   Fastenings on wooden scaffolds should conform with the national laws and regulations or be approved by the competent authority.

4.2.8.   All tubes, couplers and fittings used in metal tubular scaffolding should be of a standard and type approved by the competent authority. All couplers and fittings should be free from damage and distortion, and should be maintained in an oiled condition.

4.2.9.   Couplers should not cause deformation in tubes. Couplers should be made of drop forged steel or equivalent material.

4.2.10.   Tubes should be free from cracks, splits and excessive corrosion and be straight to the eye, and tube ends cut cleanly square with the tube axis.

4.2.11.   Alloy and steel tubing should not be intermixed on the same scaffold.

4.3. Design and construction

4.3.1.   Scaffolds should be designed for their maximum load and with a safety factor of at least 4, or as prescribed by the competent authority.

4.3.2.   Scaffolds should be adequately braced.

4.3.3.   Scaffolds which are not designed to be independent should be rigidly connected to the building at suitable vertical and horizontal distances.

4.3.4.   A scaffold should never extend above the highest anchorage to an extent which might endanger its stability and strength.

4.3.5.   Sufficient putlogs and transoms should remain in position and securely fastened to the ledgers, uprights or standards, as the case may be, to ensure the stability of the scaffold until it is finally dismantled.

4.3.6.   All scaffolds and appliances used as supports for working platforms should be of sound construction, have a firm footing, and be adequately strutted and braced to maintain their stability.

4.3.7.   Loose bricks, drainpipes, chimney-pots or other unsuitable material should not be used for the construction or support of any part of a scaffold.

4.3.8.   When necessary to prevent danger from falling objects, working platforms, gangways and stairways of scaffolds should be provided with overhead screens of adequate strength and dimensions.

4.3.9.   Nails should be driven full length, and not driven

part way and then bent over, and should not be subject to direct pull.

4.3.10. Scaffolding materials should not be thrown from scaffolds or from heights. Other materials should only be thrown from scaffolds or heights where the landing area has been designated, protected, appropriate notices displayed, and is under the supervision of a person on the landing level.

4.3.11. Metal scaffolds should not be erected in closer proximity than 5 m to overhead electricity transmission lines equipment except in accordance with safety distances laid down by the competent authority or after the electrical transmission line or equipment has been rendered electrically dead.

4.3.12. As far as practicable, every part of a working platform, gangway or stairway of a scaffold from which a person is liable to fall a distance of 2 m or as prescribed in the national laws or regulations, should be provided with guard-rails and toeboards complying with the relevant national standards.

4.3.13. Platforms on scaffolds should be of adequate dimension, especially in width, for the tasks performed from the scaffold.

4.4. Inspection and maintenance

4.4.1. Scaffolds as prescribed by national laws or regulations should be inspected, and the results recorded by a competent person:

(a) before being taken into use;

(b) at periodic intervals thereafter as prescribed for different types of scaffolds;

(c) after any alteration, interruption in use, exposure to weather or seismic conditions or any other occurrence likely to have affected their strength or stability.

4.4.2. Inspection by the competent person should more particularly ascertain that:

(a) the scaffold is of suitable type and adequate for the job;

(b) materials used in its construction are sound and of sufficient strength;

(c) it is of sound construction and stable;

(d) that the required safeguards are in position.

4.4.3. A scaffold should not be erected, substantially altered or dismantled except by or under the supervision of a competent person.

4.4.4. Every scaffold should be maintained in good and proper condition, and every part should be kept fixed or secured so that no part can be displaced in consequence of normal use.

4.4.5. No scaffold should be partly dismantled and left so that it is capable of being used, unless it continues to be safe for use.

4.5. Lifting appliances on scaffolds

4.5.1. When a lifting appliance is to be used on a scaffold:

(a) the parts of the scaffold should be carefully inspected by a competent person to determine the additional strengthening and other safety measures required;

(b) any movement of the putlogs should be prevented;

(c) if practicable, the uprights should be rigidly connected to a solid part of the building at the place where the lifting appliance is erected.

4.6. Prefabricated scaffolds

4.6.1. In the case of prefabricated scaffold systems the instructions provided by the manufacturers or suppliers should be strictly adhered to. Prefabricated scaffolds should have adequate arrangements for fixing bracing.

4.6.2. Frames of different types should not be intermingled in a single scaffold.

4.7. Use of scaffolds

4.7.1. The employer should provide competent supervision to ensure that all scaffolds are used appropriately and only for the purpose for which they are designed or erected. In transferring heavy loads on or to a scaffold a sudden shock should not be transmitted to the scaffold.

4.7.2. When necessary to prevent danger, loads being hoisted on or to scaffolds should be controlled, e.g. by a hand rope (tag line), so that they cannot strike against the scaffold.

4.7.3. The load on the scaffold should be evenly distributed, as far as practicable, and in any case should be so distributed as to avoid disturbance of the stability of the scaffold.

4.7.4. During the use of a scaffold care should constantly be taken that it is not overloaded or otherwise misused.

4.7.5. Scaffolds should not be used for the storage of material except that required for immediate use.

4.7.6. Workers should not be employed on external scaffolds in weather conditions that threaten their safety.

4.8. Suspended scaffolds

4.8.1 In addition to the requirements for scaffolds in general as regards soundness, stability and protection against the risk of falls, suspended scaffolds should meet the following specific requirements in so far as such requirements are applicable:

(a) platforms should be designed and built with dimensions that are compatible with the stability of the structure as a whole, especially the length;

(b) the number of anchorages should be compatible with the dimensions of the platform;

(c) the safety of workers should be safeguarded by an extra rope having a point of attachment independent of the anchorage arrangements of the scaffold;

(d) the anchorages and other elements of support of the scaffold should be designed and built in such a way as to ensure sufficient strength;

(e) the ropes, winches, pulleys or pulley blocks should be designed, assembled, used and maintained according to the requirements established for lifting gear adapted to the lifting of persons according to national laws and regulations;

(f) before use, the whole structure should be checked by a competent person.

5. Lifting appliances and gear

5.1. General provisions

5.1.1. Employers should have a well-planned safety programme to ensure that all the lifting appliances and lifting gear are selected, installed, examined, tested, maintained, operated and dismantled:

(a) with a view to preventing the occurrence of any accident;

(b) in accordance with the requirements laid down in the national laws, regulations and standards.

5.1.2. Every lifting appliance including its constituent elements, attachments, anchorages and supports should be of good design and construction, sound material and adequate strength for the purpose for which it is used.

5.1.3. Every lifting appliance and every item of lifting gear should be accompanied at the time of purchase with instructions for use and with a test certificate from a competent person or a guarantee of conformity with national laws and regulations concerning:

(a) the maximum safe working load;

(b) safe working loads at different radii if the lifting appliance has a variable radius;

(c) the conditions of use under which the maximum or variable safe working loads can be lifted or lowered.

5.1.4. Every lifting appliance and every item of lifting gear having a single safe working load should be clearly marked at a conspicuous place with the maximum safe working load in accordance with national laws and regulations.

5.1.5. Every lifting appliance having a variable safe working load should be fitted with a load indicator or other effective means to indicate clearly to the driver each maximum safe working load and the conditions under which it is applicable.

5.1.6. All lifting appliances should be adequately and securely supported; the weight-bearing characteristics of the ground on which the lifting appliance is to operate should be surveyed in advance of use.

Installation

5.1.7. Fixed lifting appliances should be installed:

(a) by competent persons;

(b) so that they cannot be displaced by the load, vibration or other influences;

(c) so that the operator is not exposed to danger from loads, ropes or drums;

(d) so that the operator can either see over the zone of operations or communicate with all loading and unloading points by telephone, signals or other adequate means.

5.1.8. A clearance of at least 60 cm or more, as prescribed by national laws or regulations, should be provided between moving parts or loads of lifting appliances and:

(a) fixed objects in the surrounding environment such as walls and posts; or

(b) electrical conductors.

The clearance from electrical conductors should be more for high voltages in accordance with the requirements of national laws and regulations.

5.1.9. The strength and stability of lifting appliances should take into account the effect of any wind forces to which they may be exposed.

5.1.10. No structural alterations or repairs should be made to any part of a lifting appliance which may affect the safety of the appliance without the permission and supervision of the competent person.

Examinations and tests

5.1.11. Lifting appliances and items of lifting gear, as prescribed by national laws or regulations, should be examined and tested by a competent person:

(a) before being taken into use for the first time;

(b) after erection on a site;

(c) subsequently at intervals prescribed by national laws and regulations;

(d) after any substantial alteration or repair.

5.1.12. The manner in which the examinations and tests are to be carried out by the competent person and the test loads to be applied for different types of lifting appliances and lifting gear should be in accordance with national laws and regulations.

5.1.13. The results of the examinations and tests on lifting appliances and lifting gear should be recorded in prescribed forms and, in conformity with national laws and regulations, made available to the competent authority and to employers and workers or their representatives.

Controls, control devices and cabins

5.1.14. Controls of lifting appliances should be:

(a) designed and constructed as far as possible in accordance with ergonomic principles;

(b) conveniently situated with ample room for operation and an unrestricted view for the operator;

(c) provided, where necessary, with a suitable locking device to prevent accidental movement or displacement;

(d) in a position free from danger from the passage of the load;

(e) clearly marked to show their purpose and method of operation.

5.1.15. Lifting appliances should be equipped with devices that would prevent the load from over-running and prevent the load from moving if power fails.

5.1.16. The operator of every lifting appliance used outdoors except those used for short periods should be provided with:

(a) a safe cabin with full protection from weather and adverse climatic conditions, and designed and constructed in accordance with ergonomic principles;

(b) a clear and unrestricted view of the area of operation;

(c) safe access to and egress from the cabin, including situations where the operator is taken ill.

Operation

5.1.17. No lifting appliance should be operated by a worker who:

(a) is below 18 years of age;

(b) is not medically fit;

(c) has not received appropriate training in accordance with national laws and regulations or is not properly qualified.

5.1.18. A lifting appliance or item of lifting gear should not be loaded beyond its safe working load or loads, except for testing purposes as specified by and under the direction of a competent person.

5.1.19. Where necessary to guard against danger, no lifting appliance should be used without the provision of suitable signalling arrangements or devices.

5.1.20. No person should be raised, lowered or carried by a lifting appliance unless it is constructed, installed and used for that purpose in accordance with national laws and regulations, except in an emergency situation:

(a) in which serious personal injury or fatality may occur;

(b) for which the lifting appliance can safely be used.

5.1.21.   Every part of a load in the course of being hoisted or lowered should be adequately suspended or supported so as to prevent danger.

5.1.22.   Every platform or receptacle used for hoisting bricks, tiles, slates or other loose material should be so enclosed as to prevent the fall of any of the material.

5.1.23.   Loaded wheelbarrows placed directly on a platform for raising or lowering should be taped or secured so that they cannot move and the platform should be enclosed as necessary to prevent the fall of the contents.

5.1.24.   In hoisting a barrow, the wheel should not be used as a means of lifting unless efficient steps are taken to prevent the axle from slipping out of the bearings.

5.1.25.   To avoid danger, long objects such as girders should be guided with a tag line while being raised or lowered.

5.1.26.   Landings should be so designed and arranged that workers are not obliged to lean out into empty space for loading and unloading.

5.1.27.   The hoisting of loads at points where there is a regular flow of traffic should be carried out in an enclosed space, or if this is impracticable (e.g. in the case of bulky objects), measures should be taken to hold up or divert the traffic for the time necessary.

5.2. Hoists

5.2.1.   Hoist towers should be designed according to national laws and regulations.

5.2.2. Hoist shafts should be enclosed with rigid panels or other adequate fencing:

(a) at ground level on all sides;

(b) at all other levels at all points at which access is provided;

(c) at all points at which persons are liable to be struck by any moving part.

5.2.3. The enclosure of hoist shafts, except at approaches, should extend where practicable at least 2 m above the floor, platform or other place to which access is provided except where a lesser height is sufficient to prevent any person falling down the hoistway and there is no risk of any person coming into contact with any moving part of the hoist, but in no case should the enclosure be less than 1 m in height.

5.2.4. Approaches to hoists should be provided with substantial gates or the like which:

(a) should be gridded for visibility;

(b) should, where practicable, be at least 2 m high;

(c) when closed prevent access to the hoist platform and any moving part of the hoist.

5.2.5. The guides of hoist platforms should offer sufficient resistance to bending and, in the case of jamming by a safety catch, to buckling.

5.2.6. Where necessary to prevent danger, adequate covering should be provided above the top of hoist shafts to prevent material falling down them.

5.2.7. Outdoor hoist towers should be erected on adequately firm foundations, and securely braced, guyed and anchored.

5.2.8. A suitable ladderway should extend from the bottom to the top of outdoor hoist towers, if no other ladderway exists within easy reach.

5.2.9.   Hoisting engines should be of ample capacity to control the heaviest load that they will have to move.

5.2.10.   Hoists should be provided with devices that stop the hoisting engine as soon as the platform reaches its highest stopping place.

5.2.11.   Winches should be so constructed that the brake is applied when the control handle is not held in the operating position.

5.2.12.   It should not be possible to set in motion from the platform a hoist which is not designed for the conveyance of persons.

5.2.13.   Winches should not be fitted with pawl and ratchet gears on which the pawl must be disengaged before the platform is lowered.

5.2.14.   Hoist platforms should be capable of supporting the maximum load that they will have to carry with a safety factor as laid down in national laws and regulations.

5.2.15.   Hoist platforms should be equipped with safety gear that will hold the platform with the maximum load if the hoisting rope breaks.

5.2.16.   If workers have to enter the cage or go on the platform at landings there should be a locking arrangement preventing the cage or platform from moving while any worker is in or on it.

5.2.17.   On sides not used for loading and unloading, hoist platforms should be provided with toe-boards and enclosures of wire mesh or other suitable material to prevent the fall of parts of loads.

5.2.18.   Where necessary to prevent danger from falling objects, hoist platforms should be provided with adequate covering.

5.2.19.   Counterweights consisting of an assemblage of several parts should be made of specially constructed parts rigidly connected together.

5.2.20.   Counterweights should run in guides.

5.2.21.   Suitable platforms should be provided at all landings used by workers.

5.2.22.   The following notices should be posted up conspicuously and in very legible characters:

(a) on all hoists:

  (i) on the platform: the carrying capacity in kilograms or other appropriate standard unit of weight;

  (ii) on the hoisting engine: the lifting capacity in kilograms or other appropriate standard unit of weight;

(b) on hoists authorised or certified for the conveyance of persons:

  on the platform or cage: the maximum number of persons to be carried at one time;

(c) on hoists for goods only:

  on every approach to the hoist and on the platform: prohibition of use by persons.

5.2.23.   Hoists intended for the carriage of persons should be provided with a cage so constructed as to prevent any person from falling out or being trapped between the cage and any fixed part of the structure when the cage gate is shut, or from being struck by the counterbalance weight or by articles or materials falling down the hoistway.

5.2.24.   On each side in which access is provided the cage should be fitted with a gate fitted with devices which ensure that the gate cannot be opened except when the cage is at a landing and that the gate must be closed before the cage can move away from the landing.

5.2.25.   Every gate in the enclosure of the hoist shaft which gives access from a landing place to the cage should be fitted with devices to ensure that the gate cannot be opened except when the cage is at that landing place, and that the cage cannot be moved away from that landing place until the gate is closed.

5.3. Derricks

Stiff-leg derricks

5.3.1.   Derricks should be erected on a firm base capable of taking the combined weight of the crane structure and maximum rated load.

5.3.2.   Suitable devices should be used to prevent masts from lifting out of their seatings.

5.3.3.   Electrically operated derricks should be effectively earthed from the sole-plate or framework.

5.3.4.   Counterweights should be so arranged that they do not subject the backstays, sleepers or pivots to excessive strain.

5.3.5.   When derricks are mounted on wheels:
(a) a rigid member should be used to maintain the correct distance between the wheels;
(b) they should be equipped with struts to prevent them from dropping if a wheel breaks or the derrick is derailed.

5.3.6.   The length of a derrick jib should not be altered without consulting the manufacturer.

5.3.7.   The jib of a scotch derrick crane should not be erected within the backstays of the crane.

Guy derricks

5.3.8.   The restraint of the guy ropes should be ensured by fitting stirrups or anchor plates in concrete foundations.

5.3.9.   The mast of guy derricks should be supported by six top guys spaced approximately equally.

5.3.10.   The spread of the guys of a guy derrick crane from the mast should be not more than 45 from the horizontal.

5.3.11.   Guy ropes of derricks should be equipped with a stretching screw or turnbuckle or other device to regulate the tension.

5.3.12.   Gudgeon pins, sheave pins and foot bearings should be lubricated frequently.

5.3.13.   When a derrick is not in use, the boom should be anchored to prevent it from swinging.

5.4. Gin poles

5.4.1.   Gin poles should:

(a) be straight;

(b) consist of steel or other suitable metal or straight-grained timber free from knots;

(c) be adequately guyed and anchored;

(d) be vertical or raked slightly towards the load;

(e) be of adequate strength for the loads that they will be required to move.

5.4.2.   Gin poles should not be spliced and if a gin pole is composed of different elements, they should be assembled in conformity with their intrinsic material strength.

5.4.3.   Gin poles should be adequately fastened at their feet to prevent displacement in operation.

5.4.4.   Gin poles that are moved from place to place and re-erected should not be taken into use again before the pole, lifting ropes, guys, blocks and other parts have been inspected, and the whole appliance has been tested under load.

5.4.5.   When platforms or skips are hoisted by gin poles, adequate precautions should be taken to prevent them from spinning and to provide for proper landing.

5.5. Tower cranes

5.5.1.   Where tower cranes have cabs at high level, persons should only be employed as crane operators who are capable and trained to work at heights.

5.5.2.   The characteristics of the various machines available should be considered against the operating requirements and the surroundings in which the crane will operate before a particular type of crane is selected.

5.5.3.   Care should be taken in the assessment of wind loads both during operations and out of service. Account should also be taken of the effects of high structures on wind forces in the vicinity of the crane.

5.5.4.   The ground on which the tower crane stands should have adequate bearing capacity. Account should be taken of seasonal variations in ground conditions.

5.5.5.   Bases for tower cranes and tracks for rail-mounted tower cranes should be firm and level. Tower cranes should only operate on gradients within limits specified by the manufacturer. Tower cranes should only be erected at a safe distance from excavations and ditches.

5.5.6.   Tower cranes should be sited where there is clear space available for erection, operation and dismantling. As far as possible, cranes should be sited so that loads do not have to be handled over occupied premises, over public thoroughfares, other construction works and railways or near power cables.

5.5.7. Where two or more tower cranes are sited in positions where their jibs could touch any part of the other crane, there should be direct means of communication between them and a distinct warning system operated from the cab so that one driver may alert the other to impending danger.

5.5.8. The manufacturers' instructions on the methods and sequence of erection and dismantling should be followed. The crane should be tested in accordance with national laws or regulations before being taken into use.

5.5.9. The climbing operation of climbing tower cranes should be carried out in accordance with manufacturers' instructions and national laws or regulations. The free-standing height of the tower crane should not extend beyond what is safe and is permissible in the manufacturers' instructions.

5.5.10. When the tower crane is left unattended, loads should be removed from the hook, the hook raised, the power switched off and the boom brought to the horizontal. For longer periods or at times when adverse weather conditions are expected, out of service procedures should be followed. The main jib should be slewed to the side of the tower away from the wind, put into free slew and the crane immobilised.

5.5.11. A windspeed measuring device should be provided at an elevated position on the tower crane with the indicator fitted in the drivers' cab.

5.5.12. Devices should be provided to prevent loads being moved to a point where the corresponding safe working load of the crane would be exceeded. Name boards or other items liable to catch the wind should not be mounted on a tower crane other than in accordance with the manufacturers' instructions.

5.5.13. Tower cranes should not be used for magnet, or demolition ball service, piling operations or other duties which could impose excessive loadings on the crane structure.

5.6. Lifting ropes

5.6.1. Only ropes with a known and adequate safe working capacity should be used as lifting ropes.

5.6.2. Lifting ropes should be installed, maintained and inspected in accordance with manufacturers' instuctions and national laws or regulations.

5.6.3. Repaired steel ropes should not be used on hoists.

5.6.4. Where multiple independent ropes are used, for the purpose of stability, to lift a work platform, each rope should be capable of carrying the load independently.

6. Transport, earth-moving and materials-handling equipment

6.1. General provisions

6.1.1. All vehicles and earth-moving or materials-handling equipment should:

(a) be of good design and construction taking into account as far as possible ergonomic principles particularly with reference to the seat;

(b) be maintained in good working order;

(c) be properly used with due regard to safety and health;

(d) be operated by workers who have received appropriate training in accordance with national laws and regulations.

6.1.2. The drivers and operators of vehicles and earth-moving or materials-handling equipment should be medically fit, trained and tested and of a prescribed minimum age as required by national laws and regulations.

6.1.3. On all construction sites on which vehicles, earth-moving or materials-handling equipment are used:

(a) safe and suitable access ways should be provided for them;

(b) traffic should be so organised and controlled as to secure their safe operation.

6.1.4. Adequate signalling or other control arrangements or devices should be provided to guard against danger from the movement of vehicles and earth-moving or materials-handling equipment. Special safety precautions should be taken for vehicles and equipment when manoeuvring backwards.

6.1.5. The assistance of a trained and authorised signaller should be available when the view of the driver or operator is restricted. The signalling code should be understood by all involved.

6.1.6. When earth-moving or materials-handling equipment is required to operate in dangerous proximity to live electrical conductors, adequate precautions should be taken, such as isolating the electrical supply or erecting overhead barriers of a safe height.

6.1.7. Preventive measures should be taken to avoid the fall of vehicles and earth-moving or materials-handling equipment into excavations or into water.

6.1.8. Vehicles and earth-moving or materials-handling equipment should not travel on bridges, viaducts, embankments, etc., unless it has been established that it is safe to do so.

6.1.9. Where appropriate, earth-moving or materials-handling equipment should be fitted with structures designed to protect the operator from being crushed, should the machine overturn, and from falling material.

6.1.10. All vehicles and earth-moving or materials-handling equipment should be provided with a plate or the like indicating:

(a) the gross laden weight;

(b) the maximum axle weight or, in the case of caterpillar equipment, ground pressure;

(c) the tare weight.

6.1.11. All vehicles and earth-moving or materials-handling equipment should be equipped with:

(a) an electrically operated acoustic signalling device;

(b) searchlights for forward and backward movement;

(c) power and hand brakes;

(d) tail lights;

(e) silencers;

(f) a reversing alarm.

6.1.12. Operators of vehicles and earth-moving or materials-handling equipment should be adequately protected against the weather or accidents due to impact, crushing or contact with a moving load by a cab:

(a) which is designed and constructed in accordance with ergonomic principles and provides full protection from adverse weather conditions;

(b) which is fully enclosed where dusty conditions are likely to be encountered;

(c) which provides the driver with a clear and unrestricted view of the area of operation;

(d) which is equipped with a direction indicator and a rear-view mirror on both sides.

6.1.13. The cab of vehicles and earth-moving or materials-handling equipment should be kept at least 1 m from a face being excavated.

6.1.14. When cranes and shovels are being moved, out of service, the boom should be in the direction of travel and the scoop or bucket should be raised and without load, except when travelling downhill.

6.1.15. On earth-moving and materials-handling equipment, motors, brakes, steering gear, chassis, blades, blade-holders, tracks, wire ropes, sheaves, hydraulic mechanisms, transmissions, bolts and other parts on which safety depends should be inspected daily.

6.1.16. Vehicles and earth-moving or materials-handling equipment should not be left on a slope with the engine running.

6.1.17. Deck plates and steps of vehicles and equipment should be kept free from oil, grease, mud or other slippery substances.

6.1.18. Dredge-type excavators should not be used on earth walls more than 1 m higher than the reach of the excavator if they are installed at the bottom of the wall.

6.1.19. Bucket excavators should not be used at the top or bottom of earth walls with a slope exceeding 60.

6.2. Power shovels, excavators

6.2.1. If necessary to prevent danger during inspection or repair, the jib of power shovels should be equipped with a ladder protected by a guard-rail and toe-board.

6.2.2. Brake pedals for all motions on power shovels should have two independent locking devices.

6.2.3. Power shovels should be equipped with an emergency quick-acting stop device independent of the controls.

6.2.4. Excavators that are equipped with a unit for deep digging should either be so designed that the bucket teeth cannot come nearer the boom than 40 cm or be provided with a reliable stop that prevents this from happening.

6.2.5. Excavators that are designed to be used for lifting with lifting gear should be provided with a plate in the cabin and on the boom bearing a clearly legible and durable text giving the maximum safe working load of the lifting gear fitted.

6.2.6. Excavators that are equipped for use as mobile cranes should:

(a) be examined and tested in accordance with national laws and regulations for mobile cranes;

(b) be fitted with an automatic safe working load indicator, when practicable.

43

Steam shovels

6.2.7. National laws and regulations concerning the construction, installation, operation, testing and examination of steam boilers should be followed for the boilers of steam shovels.

Internal combustion engine-operated shovels

6.2.8. Internal combustion engine-powered shovels should be:

(a) earthed or otherwise protected against static electricity;

(b) equipped with a fire extinguisher.

Electric shovels

6.2.9. The connection or disconnection of the electric cable supplying power from the transmission line to or from the electric shovel should only be done by competent persons duly authorised.

6.2.10. Electrical connectors and relays on the shovel should be inspected daily if in operation.

Operation of power shovels

6.2.11. The boom should be prevented from accidentally swinging during operation or transport.

6.2.12. The bucket or grab of a power shovel should be prevented from accidentally dipping, tipping or swinging in operation.

6.2.13. Before leaving the shovel the operator should:

(a) disengage the master clutch;

(b) lower the bucket or grab to the ground.

6.2.14. Buckets and grabs of power shovels should be propped to restrict movement while they are being repaired or teeth are being changed.

6.2.15. When an excavator is at work near a wall or similar construction, persons should be prevented from entering the danger zone in which they may be crushed when the machine turns.

6.2.16. Trucks should not be loaded in any place where there may be danger from materials such as rocks falling from buckets passing overhead; where this cannot be avoided, no person should remain in the cab during loading.

6.2.17. Trucks should be stationed at such a distance from the excavator that there is a clearance of at least 60 cm between the truck and the superstructure of the excavator even when it turns.

6.2.18. While work is being done on hydraulically operated buckets the piston should be fully drawn back in the hydraulic cylinder, and where necessary props provided.

6.3. Bulldozers

6.3.1. Before leaving a bulldozer the operator should:

(a) apply the brakes;

(b) lower the blade and ripper;

(c) put the shift lever in neutral.

6.3.2. At the close of work bulldozers should be left on level ground.

6.3.3. When a bulldozer is moving uphill the blade should be kept low.

6.3.4. Bulldozer blades should not be used as brakes except in an emergency.

6.4. Scrapers

6.4.1. The tractor and scrapers should be joined by a safety line when in operation.

6.4.2. Scraper bowls should be propped while blades are being replaced.

6.4.3. Scrapers moving downhill should be left in gear.

6.5. Mobile asphalt layers and finishers

6.5.1. Wooden floors in front of the sprayers should be covered with corrugated sheet metal.

6.5.2. The mixer elevator should be within a wooden or sheet-metal enclosure which should have a window for observation, lubrication and maintenance.

6.5.3. Bitumen scoops should have adequate covers.

6.5.4. The sprayer should be provided with a fire-resisting shield with an observation window.

6.5.5. To avoid fire risks due to foaming:

(a) boilers should have a device that prevents foam from reaching the burners; or

(b) only non-foaming products should be used.

6.5.6. When asphalt plants are working on public roads, an adequate traffic control system should be established and reflective jackets provided for the workers.

6.5.7. A sufficient number of fire extinguishers should be kept in readiness on the worksite, including at least two on the spreader.

6.5.8. Material should only be loaded on to the elevator after the drying drum has warmed up.

6.5.9.   No naked flame should be used for ascertaining the level of asphalt in the tank.

6.5.10.   Thinners (cut-backs) should not be heated over an open flame.

6.5.11.   If a burner flame is extinguished:

(a) the fuel supply should be cut off;

(b) the heating tube should be thoroughly blown out by the fan so as to prevent a backfire.

6.5.12.   Inspection openings should not be opened while there is any pressure in the boiler.

6.6. Pavers

6.6.1.   Pavers should be equipped with guards that prevent workers from walking under the skip.

6.7. Road rollers

6.7.1.   Before a road roller is used the ground should be examined for bearing capacity and general safety, especially at the edges of slopes such as embankments.

6.7.2.   Rollers should not move downhill with the engine out of gear.

6.7.3.   When a roller is not in use:

(a) the brakes should be applied;

(b) the engine should be put into bottom gear if the roller is facing uphill;

(c) the engine should be put into reverse if the roller is facing downhill;

(d) the contact should be switched off;

(e) the wheels should be blocked.

7. Plant, machinery, equipment and hand tools

7.1. General provisions

7.1.1. Plant, machinery and equipment, including hand tools, both manual and power-driven, should:

(a) be of good design and construction, taking into account, as far as possible, health and safety and ergonomic principles;

(b) be maintained in good working order;

(c) be used only for work for which they have been designed unless a use outside the initial design purpose has been assessed by a competent person who has concluded that such use is safe;

(d) be operated only by workers who have been authorised and given appropriate training;

(e) be provided with protective guards, shields, or other devices as required by national laws or regulations.

7.1.2. Adequate instructions for safe use should be provided where appropriate by the manufacturer or the employer, in a form understood by the user.

7.1.3. As far as practicable, safe operating procedures should be established and used for all plant, machinery and equipment.

7.1.4. Operators of plant, machinery and equipment should not be distracted while work is in progress.

7.1.5. Plant, machinery and equipment should be switched off when not in use and isolated before any major adjustment, cleaning or maintenance is done.

7.1.6. Where trailing cables or hose pipes are used they should be kept as short as practicable and not allowed to create a safety hazard.

7.1.7. All dangerous moving parts of machinery and equipment should be enclosed or adequately guarded in accordance with national laws and regulations.

7.1.8. Every power-driven machine and equipment should be provided with adequate means, immediately accessible and readily identifiable to the operator, of stopping it quickly and preventing it from being started again inadvertently.

7.1.9. The machines or equipment should be so designed or fitted with a device that the maximum safe speed, which should be indicated on it, is not exceeded. If the speed of the machine is variable, it should only be possible to start it at the lowest speed appropriate.

7.1.10. Operators of plant, machinery, equipment and tools should be provided with personal protective equipment including, where necessary, suitable hearing protection.

7.2. Hand tools

7.2.1. Hand tools and implements should be tempered, dressed and repaired by competent persons.

7.2.2. The cutting edges of cutting tools should be kept sharp.

7.2.3. Heads of hammers and other shock tools should be dressed or ground to a suitable radius on the edge as soon as they begin to mushroom or crack.

7.2.4. When not in use and while being carried or transported sharp tools should be kept in sheaths, shields, chests or other suitable containers.

7.2.5.   Only insulated or non-conducting tools should be used on or near live electrical installations if there is any risk of electrical shock.

7.2.6.   Only non-sparking tools should be used near or in the presence of flammable or explosive dusts or vapours.

7.3. Pneumatic tools

7.3.1.   Operating triggers on portable pneumatic tools should be:

(a) so placed as to minimise the risk of accidental starting of the machine;

(b) so arranged as to close the air inlet valve automatically when the pressure of the operator's hand is removed.

7.3.2.   Hose and hose connections for compressed-air supply to portable pneumatic tools should be:

(a) designed for the pressure and service for which they are intended;

(b) fastened securely to the pipe outlet and equipped with a safety chain, as appropriate.

7.3.3.   Pneumatic shock tools should be equipped with safety clips or retainers to prevent dies and tools from being accidentally expelled from the barrel.

7.3.4.   Pneumatic tools should be disconnected from power and the pressure in hose lines released before any adjustments or repairs are made.

7.4. Cartridge-operated tools

7.4.1.   Whenever practicable, a low-velocity tool should be used.

7.4.2. Cartridge-operated tools should have:

(a) a guard or protective shield that cannot be removed without rendering the tool inoperative;

(b) a device that prevents the tool from firing inadvertently, for example if it is dropped or while it is being loaded;

(c) a device that prevents the tool from firing if it is not approximately perpendicular to the working surface;

(d) a device that prevents the tool from firing if the muzzle is not pressed against the working surface.

7.4.3. The recoil of a cartridge-operated tool should not be capable of injuring the user.

7.4.4. The noise of the detonation should not be such as to damage hearing.

7.4.5. A cartridge-operated tool, before each occasion of use, should be inspected to ensure that it is safe to use, and in particular:

(a) that the safety devices are in proper working order;

(b) that the tool is clean;

(c) that all moving parts work easily;

(d) that the barrel is unobstructed.

7.4.6. At intervals recommended by the manufacturer the tool should be completely dismantled and inspected for wear on the safety devices by a competent person.

7.4.7. Cartridge-operated tools should only be repaired by the manufacturer or by competent persons.

7.4.8. Cartridges should not be stored nor cartridge tools operated:

(a) in a place or environment where these could explode accidentally;

(b) in an explosive atmosphere.

7.4.9. When not required for use, inspection or other purpose, cartridge-operated tools should be kept in a suitable container that:

(a) is made of suitable material;

(b) is clearly marked to indicate its contents;

(c) is kept locked when not in use;

(d) contains nothing except the tools and cartridges.

7.4.10. No cartridge-operated tool should be stored or transported loaded, or left loaded when not in use.

7.4.11. Cartridge-operated tools should be accompanied by instructions for their maintenance and use and should only be operated by persons trained in their safe use.

7.5. Electrical tools

7.5.1. Portable electrical tools should generally be used on reduced voltage to avoid as far as possible the risk of a lethal shock.

7.5.2. All electrical tools should be earthed, unless they are "all insulated" or "double insulated" tools which do not require an earth. Earthing should be incorporated in metallic cases, and as a safeguard against damaged cables where wires enter the tool.

7.5.3. All electrical tools should receive inspection and maintenance on a regular basis by a competent electrician, and complete records kept.

7.6. Woodworking machines

7.6.1. Shavings, sawdust, etc, should not be removed by hand from woodworking machines or in their vicinity while the machines are working.

7.6.2. Where provided, chip and sawdust extraction systems should be maintained in efficient working order.

7.6.3. Mechanical feeding devices should be used whenever practicable.

7.6.4. All cutters and saw blades should be enclosed as far as practicable.

7.6.5. Circular saws should be provided with strong, rigid and easily adjustable hood guards for the saw blades and with riving knives of suitable design matched to the saw blade in use. The width of the opening in the table for the saw blade should be as small as practicable.

7.6.6. Portable circular saws should be so designed that when the blade is running idle it is automatically covered.

7.6.7. On band saws all the blade, except the operating portion, should be enclosed. Band wheels should be enclosed with stout guards.

7.6.8. Band saws should be provided with automatic tension regulators.

7.6.9. Planing machines should be provided with bridge guards covering the full length and breadth of the cutting block and easily adjustable in both horizontal and vertical directions.

7.6.10. Thicknessing machines should be provided with sectional feed rollers or a kick-back preventer which should be kept as free as possible.

7.6.11. Woodworking machines should be properly spaced to avoid accidental injury when handling large boards or long planks.

7.7. Engines

7.7.1.   Engines should:

(a) be constructed and installed so that they can be started safely and the maximum safe speed cannot be exceeded;

(b) have remote controls for limiting speed when necessary;

(c) have devices to stop them from a safe place in an emergency.

7.7.2.   Internal combustion engines should not run for long periods in confined spaces unless adequate exhaust ventilation is provided.

7.7.3.   When internal combustion engines are being fuelled:

(a) the engine ignition should be shut off;

(b) care should be taken to avoid spilling fuel;

(c) no person should smoke or have an open light in the vicinity;

(d) a fire extinguisher should be kept readily available.

7.7.4   Secondary fuel reservoirs should be placed outside the engine room.

7.8. Silos

7.8.1.   Silos should:

(a) be erected on adequate foundations;

(b) withstand the stresses to which they are subjected without any deformation of walls, floors and other load-bearing parts.

7.8.2.   All places in silos to which workers have to go should be provided with safe means of access such as stairs, fixed ladders or hoists.

7.8.3. Facilities should be provided to enable the quantity of material in the silo to be assessed without entering the silo.

7.8.4. On silos, notices should be conspicuously displayed:

(a) containing details of the requirements for entry;

(b) calling attention to the danger of sinking in fine materials.

7.8.5. If the material in the silo is liable to cause a blockage, agitators, compressed air or other mechanical devices should be preferably provided. To clear blockages, equipment such as poles, long-handled tools, rammers or scraper chains should also be available for emergency use.

7.8.6. Silos for material liable to spontaneous combustion should be provided with fire-extinguishing equipment.

7.8.7. In silos in which explosive mixtures of gases or dusts are liable to form:

(a) all electrical equipment including hand lamps should be flameproof;

(b) only non-sparking tools should be used;

(c) explosion vents should be provided in the walls.

7.8.8. Entrances of silos should be kept closed and locked.

7.8.9. Workers should not enter a silo unless:

(a) the discharge opening is closed and secured against opening and filling is stopped;

(b) they are duly authorised to do so;

(c) they wear safety harnesses with lifelines securely attached to a fixed object;

(d) another authorised person provides constant surveillance and is in attendance with suitable rescue equipment.

7.9. Concrete work equipment

7.9.1. Concrete mixers should be protected by side railings to prevent workers from passing under the skip while it is raised.

7.9.2. Hoppers into which a person could fall, and revolving blades of trough or batch-type mixers, should be adequately guarded by grating.

7.9.3. In addition to the operating brake, skips of concrete mixers should be provided with a device or devices by which they can be securely blocked when raised.

7.9.4. While the drum of a concrete mixer is being cleaned, adequate precautions should be taken to protect the workers inside by locking switches open, removing fuses or otherwise cutting off the power.

7.9.5. Concrete buckets for use with cranes and aerial cableways should be free as far as practicable from projections from which accumulations of concrete could fall.

7.9.6. Loaded concrete buckets should be guided into position by appropriate means.

7.9.7. Concrete buckets positioned by crane or aerial cableways should be suspended by safety hooks.

7.9.8. When concrete is being tipped from buckets, workers should keep out of range of any kick-back due to concrete sticking to the bucket.

7.9.9. Concrete bucket towers and masts with pouring gutters or conveyor belts should:

(a) be erected by competent persons;

(b) be inspected daily.

7.9.10. The winch for hoisting the bucket should be so placed that the operator can see the filling, hoisting, emptying and lowering of the bucket. Where this is not practicable, a banksman should direct the operator.

7.9.11. If the winch operator cannot see the bucket, he should, where practicable, be provided with an adequate means indicating its position.

7.9.12. Guides for the bucket should be correctly aligned and so maintained as to prevent the bucket from jamming in the tower.

7.9.13. Scaffolding carrying a pipe for pumped concrete should be strong enough to support the pipe when filled and all the workers who may be on the scaffold at the same time, with a safety factor of at least 4.

7.9.14. Pipes for carrying pumped concrete should:

(a) be securely anchored at the ends and at curves;

(b) be provided near the top with air release valves;

(c) be securely attached to the pump nozzle by a bolted collar or equivalent means.

7.10. Pressure plant

7.10.1. Pressure plant and equipment should be examined, tested and issued with a certificate by a competent person in cases and at times prescribed by national laws or regulations.

7.10.2. National laws or regulations should be laid down and enforced as regards the materials, design, construction, installation, inspection, testing, maintenance and operation of steam boilers and other pressure plant as necessary.

7.10.3. Only persons tested and certified by the competent authorities should operate steam boilers.

7.10.4.   Compressors should be equipped with:

(a) automatic devices that will prevent the maximum safe discharge pressure from being exceeded;

(b) a quick-release valve;

(c) suitable arrangements for preventing contamination where persons are working in confined spaces.

7.10.5.   Compressors in which explosive mixtures of gas may form should be protected against sparking.

7.10.6.   Where compressor cylinders are equipped with water-cooling jackets it should be possible to observe the water flow.

7.10.7.   Intercoolers and aftercoolers should be able to withstand safely the maximum pressure in the air-discharge piping.

7.10.8.   Where necessary to prevent danger, air-discharge piping of compressors should be provided with:

(a) a fusible plug;

(b) insulating covers to protect workers against burns, and to prevent fire risks.

7.10.9.   Where necessary to prevent danger, an oil separator should be provided between the compressor and the air receiver.

7.10.10.   Where stop valves are installed in air-discharge piping:

(a) they should be easily accessible for inspection and cleaning;

(b) one or more safety valves should be installed between the compressor and the stop valve.

7.10.11.   All working parts, including speed governors, safety valves and oil separators, should be inspected and cleaned at suitable intervals.

7.10.12.   Air receivers should be equipped with:

(a) a safety valve;

(b) a pressure gauge;

(c) a drain cock.

7.10.13.   Air receivers should be provided with suitable openings for inspection and cleaning.

7.10.14.   Air receivers should be examined and tested at appropriate intervals by a competent person.

7.10.15.   The safe working pressure should be marked in a distinctive colour on the pressure gauge.

7.10.16.   Where necessary to prevent danger, a pressure-reducing valve or a stop valve, or both, should be inserted in the piping between the air receiver and the compressor.

7.10.17.   Between the receiver and each consuming appliance there should be a stop valve.

7.10.18.   Cylinders for compressed, dissolved or liquefied gases should be properly constructed with sound material, fitted with appropriate safety devices in accordance with national laws or regulations, inspected and tested by a competent person as prescribed and stored, transported, handled and used in conformity with the prescribed safety measures.

7.11. Conveyors

7.11.1.   Conveyors should be so constructed and installed as to avoid hazardous points between moving and stationary parts or objects.

7.11.2.   When conveyors that are not entirely enclosed cross over places where workers are employed or pass beneath, sheet or screen guards should be provided to catch any falling material. Adequate fencing should be provided at transfer points.

Emergency stopping devices should be fitted at convenient locations easily accessible for workers.

7.11.3. Power-driven conveyors should be provided at loading and unloading stations, at drive and take-up ends, and at other convenient places, if necessary to prevent danger, with devices for stopping the conveyor machinery in an emergency.

7.11.4. Where two or more conveyors are operated together, the controlling devices should be so arranged that no conveyor can feed on to a stopped conveyor.

7.11.5. Screw conveyors should be enclosed at all times. The cover should not be removed until the conveyor is stopped.

7.11.6. When a conveyor is discharging into a bunker or hopper, the feeding conveyor should be equipped with an overload switch.

7.12. Crusher plants

7.12.1. Crusher plants should be located at a safe distance from the construction work area to avoid injury to workers and damage to the workers resulting from dust, sand, gravel, noise and vibrations.

7.12.2. Crusher plants should be provided with an overriding power isolation switch next to the crusher unit and visible from it, to prevent starting the plant inadvertently during repair or maintenance.

7.12.3. Electrical motors, switches, connections and all instrumentation should be dust and moisture proof.

7.12.4. Equipment, plant and machinery should be cleared daily of dust and sand.

7.12.5. Access roads to the crusher hopper and screens should be cleaned by water spraying or other effective means.

7.12.6. Power cables should be laid out either underground or at safe elevation and marked with bright colour indicators to avoid damage resulting from poor visibility.

7.12.7. Earth-moving equipment working at a crusher plant should be cleaned and maintained after each work shift.

7.13. Power generators

7.13.1. Power generators should meet national laws and regulations for safe and reliable operation.

7.13.2. Power generators should be rated to meet the maximum anticipated load.

7.13.3. Power generators should be located in enclosed and properly ventilated areas.

7.13.4. Power generators should be provided with an overriding power switch to avoid accidental remote starting during maintenance.

7.13.5. Power generators should be provided with adequate silencers and exhaust piping.

7.13.6. When located near workers' accommodation, power generators should be housed in a concrete room or properly insulated area in accordance with national laws and regulations to minimise noise disturbance.

8. Work at heights including roof work

8.1. General provisions

8.1.1.   Where necessary to guard against danger, or where the height of a structure or its slope exceeds that prescribed by national laws or regulations, preventive measures should be taken against the fall of workers and tools or other objects or materials.

8.1.2.   Elevated workplaces, including roofs more than 2 m or as prescribed, above the floor or ground should be protected on all open sides by guard-rails and toe-boards complying with the relevant national laws and regulations. Wherever guard-rails and toe-boards cannot be provided, adequate safety harnesses should be provided and used.

8.1.3.   Elevated workplaces including roofs should be provided with safe means of access and egress such as stairs, ramps or ladders complying with the relevant national laws and regulations.

8.1.4.   If guard-rails are not practicable, persons employed at elevated workplaces including roofs from which they are liable to fall more than 2 m or as prescribed should be protected by means of adequate safety nets or safety sheets or platforms, or be secured by safety harnesses with lifelines securely attached.

8.2. Roof work

8.2.1.   All roof-work operations should be pre-planned and properly supervised.

8.2.2.   Roof work should only be undertaken by workers

who are physically and psychologically fit and have the necessary knowledge and experience for such work.

8.2.3.   Work on roofs should not be carried on in weather conditions that threaten the safety of workers.

8.2.4.   Crawling boards, walkways and roof ladders should be securely fastened to a firm structure.

8.2.5.   Roofing brackets should fit the slope of the roof and be securely supported.

8.2.6.   Where it is necessary for a person to kneel or crouch near the edge of the roof an intermediate rail should be provided unless other precautions, such as the use of a safety harness, are taken.

8.2.7.   On a large roof where work does not have to be carried out at or near the edge, a simple barrier consisting of crossed scaffold tubes supporting a tubing guard-rail may be provided. Such barriers should be positioned at least 2 m from the edge.

8.2.8.   All covers for openings in roofs should be of substantial construction and be secured in position.

8.2.9.   Roofs with a pitch of more than 10 should be treated as sloping.

8.2.10.   When work is being carried out on sloping roofs, sufficient and suitable crawling boards or roof ladders should be provided and firmly secured in position as soon as is practicable.

8.2.11.   During extensive work on the roof, strong barriers or guard-rails and toe-boards should be provided to stop a person from falling off the roof.

8.2.12.   Where workers are required to work on or near roofs or other places covered with fragile material, through which they are liable to fall, they should be provided with sufficient suitable roof ladders or crawling boards strong enough, when spanning across the supports for the roof covering, to support those workers.

8.2.13.   A minimum of two boards should be provided so that it is not necessary for a person to stand on a fragile roof to move a board or a ladder, or for any other reason.

8.2.14.   To prevent danger, suitable material such as steel wire mesh should be placed in position before any roof sheeting of asbestos cement or other fragile material is placed upon it.

8.2.15.   Purlins or other intermediate supports for fragile roofing material should be sufficiently close together to prevent danger.

8.2.16.   Where a valley or parapet gutter of a fragile roof is used for access, protection against falling through the fragile material should be provided by covering the adjacent fragile material to a minimum distance of 1 m up the roof.

8.2.17.   Buildings with fragile roofs should have a warning notice prominently displayed at the approaches to the roof.

8.3. Work on tall chimneys

8.3.1.   For the erection and repair of tall chimneys, appropriate scaffolding should be provided. An adequate catch net should be maintained at a suitable distance below the scaffold.

8.3.2.   The scaffold floor should always be at least 65 cm below the top of the chimney.

8.3.3.   Under the working floor of the scaffolding the next lower floor should be left in position as a catch platform.

8.3.4.   The distance between the inside edge of the scaffold and the wall of the chimney should not exceed 20 cm at any point.

8.3.5.   Catch platforms should be erected over:

(a) the entrance to the chimney;

(b) passageways and working places where workers could be endangered by falling objects.

8.3.6.   For climbing tall chimneys, access should be provided by:

(a) stairs or ladders;

(b) a column of iron rungs securely embedded in the chimney wall;

(c) other appropriate means.

8.3.7.   When workers use the outside rungs to climb the chimney, a securely fastened steel core rope looped at the free end and hanging down at least 3 m should be provided at the top to help the workers to climb on to the chimney.

8.3.8.   While work is being done on independent chimneys the area surrounding the chimney should be enclosed by fencing at a safe distance.

8.3.9.   Workers employed on the construction, alteration, maintenance or repair of tall chimneys should not:

(a) work on the outside without a safety harness attached by a lifeline to a rung, ring or other secure anchorage;

(b) put tools between the safety harness and the body or in pockets not intended for the purpose;

(c) haul heavy materials or equipment up and down by hand to or from the workplace on the chimney;

(d) fasten pulleys or scaffolding to reinforcing rings without first verifying their stability;

(e) work alone;

(f) climb a chimney that is not provided with securely anchored ladders or rungs;

(g) work on chimneys in use unless the necessary precautions to avoid danger from smoke and gases have been taken.

8.3.10. Work on independent chimneys should not be carried on in high winds, icy conditions, fog or during electrical storms.

9. Excavations, shafts, earthworks, underground works and tunnels

9.1. General provisions

9.1.1. Adequate precautions should be taken in any excavation, shaft, earthworks, underground works or tunnel:

(a) by suitable shoring or otherwise, to guard against danger to workers from a fall or dislodgement of earth, rock or other material;

(b) to guard against dangers arising from the fall of persons, materials or objects or the inrush of water into the excavation, shaft, earthworks, underground works or tunnel;

(c) to secure adequate ventilation at every workplace so as to maintain an atmosphere fit for respiration and to limit any fumes, gases, vapours, dust or other impurities to levels which are not dangerous or injurious to health and are within limits laid down by national laws or regulations;

(d) to enable the workers to reach safety in the event of fire, or an inrush of water or material;

(e) to avoid risk to workers arising from possible underground dangers such as the circulation of fluids or the presence of pockets of gas, by undertaking appropriate investigations to locate them.

9.1.2. Shoring or other support for any part of an excavation, shaft, earthworks, underground works or tunnel should not be erected, altered or dismantled except under the supervision of a competent person.

9.1.3. Every part of an excavation, shaft, earthworks, underground works and tunnel where persons are employed should be inspected by a competent person at times and in cases prescribed by national laws or regulations, and the results recorded.

9.1.4. Work should not commence therein until the inspection by the competent person as prescribed by national laws or regulations has been carried out and the part of the excavation, shaft, earthworks, underground works or tunnel has been found safe for work.

9.2. Excavations

9.2.1. Before digging begins on site:

(a) all excavation work should be planned and the method of excavation and the type of support work required decided;

(b) the stability of the ground should be verified by a competent person;

(c) a competent person should check that the excavation will not affect adjoining buildings, structures or roadways;

(d) the employer should verify the position of all the public utilities such as underground sewers, gas pipes, water pipes and electrical conductors that may cause danger during work;

(e) if necessary to prevent danger, the gas, water, electrical and other public utilities should be shut off or disconnected;

(f) if underground pipes, cable conductors, etc., cannot be removed or disconnected, they should be fenced, hung up and adequately marked or otherwise protected;

(g) the position of bridges, temporary roads and spoil heaps should be determined;

(h) if necessary to prevent danger, land should be cleared of trees, boulders and other obstructions;

(i) the employer should see that the land to be excavated is not contaminated by harmful chemicals or gases, or by any hazardous waste material such as asbestos.

9.2.2. All excavation work should be supervised by a competent person and operatives doing the work should be given clear instructions.

9.2.3. Sides of excavations should be thoroughly inspected:

(a) daily, prior to each shift and after interruption in work of more than one day;

(b) after every blasting operation;

(c) after an unexpected fall of ground;

(d) after substantial damage to supports;

(e) after a heavy rain, frost or snow;

(f) when boulder formations are encountered.

9.2.4. No load, plant or equipment should be placed or moved near the edge of any excavation where it is likely to cause its collapse and thereby endanger any person unless precautions such as the provision of shoring or piling are taken to prevent the sides from collapsing.

9.2.5. Adequately anchored stop blocks and barriers should be provided to prevent vehicles being driven into the excavation. Heavy vehicles should not be allowed near the excavation unless the support work has been specially designed to permit it.

9.2.6. If an excavation is likely to affect the security of a structure on which persons are working, precautions should be taken to protect the structure from collapse.

9.2.7. Sides of excavations where workers are exposed to danger from moving ground should be made safe by sloping, shoring, portable shields or other effective means.

9.2.8. All support work should be regularly checked to ensure that the props, wedges, etc., are tight and no undue deflection or distortion is taking place.

9.2.9.   All timber subject to the varying weather conditions should be regularly checked for dryness, shrinkage and rot.

9.3. Underground construction

9.3.1. General provisions

9.3.1.1.   Underground construction work should be carried on in accordance with plans approved by the competent authority when required by national laws and regulations. The plant should define excavation methods, rescue and evacuation methods in case of fire, flood and fall or dislodgement of earth or rock.

9.3.1.2.   All underground construction work should be supervised by a competent person and operatives doing the work should be given clear instructions.

9.3.1.3.   All occupied workplaces underground should be inspected at least once in every shift.

9.3.1.4.   Places occupied by solitary workers should be inspected at least twice in every shift.

9.3.1.5.   At least once in every week, thorough inspection should be made of all machinery, equipment, structures, supports, roadways, means of egress, magazines, medical facilities, sanitation and working places.

9.3.1.6.   All workers should be withdrawn from underground workings if:

(a) the ventilation fails; or

(b) other imminent danger threatens.

9.3.1.7.   A suitable communication system should be maintained from the vicinity of the face of underground workings to the surface with stations at intermediate workplaces.

9.3.1.8. In tunnels and other underground workings where an explosive mixture such as methane and air may form, operations should be carried on in accordance with national laws and regulations applicable to gassy mines or coal mines.

9.3.1.9. Air should be tested to ascertain if it is hazardous and no one allowed entry until it is fit for breathing.

9.3.1.10. Escape routes should be properly indicated with signs visible in dim light.

9.3.2. Shaft sinking

9.3.2.1. Every shaft not sunk through solid rock should be cased, lined or otherwise made safe.

9.3.2.2. Shuttering for masonry lining of shafts should only be removed gradually as the masonry progresses.

9.3.2.3. Workers employed on sinking shafts should be provided with staging, scaffolds or cradles from which they can work safely.

9.3.2.4. A thorough inspection of the shaft should be made:

(a) before a shift descends;

(b) after blasting.

9.3.2.5. All shafts over 30 m in depth should have an adequate head frame strong enough to withstand safely the maximum load that it will have to carry and preferably be of open steelwork construction.

9.3.2.6. If head frames are of timber, they should be treated to make them fire-resistant.

9.3.2.7. Head frames should be earthed or otherwise adequately protected against lightning.

9.3.2.8. All landings in shafts should be provided with

gates that effectively close the opening to a height of at least 2 m.

9.3.2.9.   Shafts should be equipped with a signalling system that warns the hoisting engineer when a conveyance passes beyond the safe limit of travel.

9.3.2.10.   Before tunnelling operations are begun from a shaft, two separate signalling or communications systems of different types should be installed.

9.3.2.11.   The signal code should be posted in the hoisting machine room and at each landing.

9.3.2.12.   Hoisting machines should be equipped:

(a) with an adequate brake that will automatically stop and hold the conveyance if the hoisting power fails;

(b) with a reliable depth indicator.

9.3.2.13.   All hoisting machines should be inspected at least once a day by the hoisting engineer.

9.3.2.14.   Shafts exceeding 30 m in depth should have an installation for conveying persons.

9.3.2.15.   Cages or cars for conveying persons should be equipped with safety gear that automatically holds the cage or car when fully loaded if the suspension rope breaks or becomes slack.

9.3.2.16.   There should be adequate means of blocking the cage or car at every landing.

9.3.2.17.   Buckets used for conveying persons in shafts should:

(a) have no projections on the outside that could catch in an obstruction;

(b) be not less than 1 m deep;

(c) be provided with adequate means to prevent them from inadvertently tipping and spinning;

(*d*) not be self-opening.

9.3.2.18. Notices should be posted at conspicuous places at the hoisting installation stating:

(*a*) the maximum speed for transporting persons in the shaft;

(*b*) the maximum number of persons and the maximum weight of material that may be safely carried in each conveyance.

9.3.2.19. Hoisting operations in shafts should be governed by suitable signals.

9.3.3. Ventilation

9.3.3.1. All underground workings should be traversed by a regular air current to keep them in a fit state for working and, in particular:

(*a*) to avoid excessive rises in temperature;

(*b*) to dilute harmful dusts, gases, vapours and fumes to safe concentrations;

(*c*) to prevent the oxygen content of the atmosphere from falling below 17 per cent or a level prescribed in national laws and regulations.

9.3.3.2. In all underground workings it should be possible to reverse the air flow.

9.3.3.3. In tunnels where blasting is done:

(*a*) an adequate supply of air should be taken to the face by mechanical ventilation;

(*b*) after every blast the face should be cleared of harmful gases and dust as far as practicable by exhaust ventilation; where necessary, the dust should be controlled with water sprays or fog guns;

(*c*) if necessary to remove the fumes, auxiliary ventilation should be provided.

9.3.3.4. Where adequate ventilation is not possible, workers should be provided with suitable breathing apparatus. Only in very exceptional circumstances should people be allowed to work without adequate ventilation.

9.3.4. Fire protection

9.3.4.1. No combustible structure should be built or any flammable material stored within 30 m of a shaft, tunnel mouth, hoisting-engine house or ventilation-fan house.

9.3.4.2. As far as practicable, combustible materials and flammable liquids should not be stored underground.

9.3.4.3. Lubricating oils, grease and rope dressings underground should:

(a) be kept in closed metal containers;

(b) be stored in a safe place away from shafts, hoists, explosives and timber.

9.3.4.4. Unless there is no risk of fire or explosion, naked lights and smoking should not be allowed underground.

9.3.4.5. Petrol engines should not be used underground except under conditions approved by the competent authority.

9.3.4.6. If welding or flame cutting is done underground:

(a) timber supports and other combustible structures or materials should be protected by a fireproof screen;

(b) suitable fire extinguishers should be kept readily available;

(c) a constant watch should be kept for outbreaks of fire;

(d) welding fumes should be removed by exhaust ventilation.

9.3.5. Electricity

9.3.5.1. Electrical installations in shafts and tunnels should comply with the relevant national laws or regulations.

9.3.5.2. Main switchgear for cutting off the supply of electricity from all underground installations should:

(a) be installed on the surface;

(b) be accessible only to authorised persons;

(c) be attended by a competent person authorised to operate it.

9.3.5.3. Where necessary suitable lightning arresters should be installed on the surface to protect the installation below ground from abnormal voltage due to atmospheric electricity.

9.3.5.4. The main cables supplying current to electric motors installed in the vicinity of shafts (such as those for underground fans or drainage pumps) should be duplicated if the stopping of these motors would cause danger.

9.3.5.5. All switches should be of the enclosed safety type.

9.3.5.6. Fixed lamps underground should be provided with a strong protective cover of glass or other transparent material or with a guard.

9.3.5.7. Whenever required by local conditions, lamp fittings should be proof against dust, gases and water.

9.3.5.8. The voltage of hand lamps (portable lamps) used underground should not exceed extra-low safety voltage.

9.3.6. Underground lighting

9.3.6.1. All places where workers have to work or pass should be adequately lit.

9.3.6.2. In addition to the main lighting, there should be emergency lighting that functions long enough to enable the workers to reach the surface safely.

75

9.4. Drilling

9.4.1.   When drilling is done in rock, loose rock should be scaled down to protect drillers against falls of ground; where this is not practicable, a protective canopy or overhead screen should be provided.

9.5. Transport, storage and handling of explosives

9.5.1.   The transport, storage and handling of explosives should comply with the requirements of national laws and regulations.

9.5.2.   Explosives should not be conveyed in a shaft cage or bucket together with other materials.

9.5.3.   Explosives and detonators should not be conveyed together in a shaft unless they are in a suitable powder car.

9.6. Blasting

9.6.1.   The modes of blasting should be in accordance with national laws or regulations.

9.6.2.   No other electrical circuit should be installed on the same side of the tunnel as the blasting circuit.

9.6.3.   Before any shot is fired, all electrical circuits other than the blasting circuit should be de-energised within an adequate distance from the firing point.

9.6.4.   Only suitable battery lamps should be used during loading shotholes.

9.6.5.   After every blast, the sides, workface and roof should be inspected and cleared of loose rock.

9.7. Haulage

9.7.1.   The haulage system should comply with the national laws and regulations.

9.7.2.   In tunnels where there are rail tracks, unless there is adequate clearance between the rolling stock and the sides, recesses should be provided at suitable intervals which should be large enough to accommodate two persons and should be at least 60 cm deep.

9.7.3.   Mechanical haulage operations should be controlled by suitable signals.

9.7.4.   Trains and single cars should have headlights and tail-lights.

9.7.5.   Rerailing by hauling with a winch should only be done under the control and supervision of a competent person.

9.7.6.   Workers should not be transported on locomotives or in cars other than those specially provided for that purpose.

9.8. Dust control

9.8.1.   Adequate measures should be taken to prevent the formation of, or to suppress as close to the source as practicable, all dust in tunnelling operations and in particular siliceous dusts consisting of particles less than 5 microns in size.

9.8.2.   If drilling in rock is done dry, the dust produced should be effectively exhausted and collected.

9.8.3.   If drilling in rock is done wet, the drill should be so constructed that it cannot be operated unless the water feed is operating.

9.8.4.   During blasting, before any shots are fired the floor, roof and sides in the vicinity should be thoroughly wetted, if practicable.

9.8.5.   Loose rock should be adequately wetted during loading, transport and unloading underground.

9.8.6.   Excavated material should not be exposed to high-velocity air currents during transport.

9.8.7.   If any stone-crushing equipment is used underground, adequate measures should be taken to prevent any dust from it penetrating to areas occupied by workers.

9.9. Underground pipelines

9.9.1.   Adequate ventilation should be provided for workers in pipelines.

9.9.2.   When laying pipes in water-bearing ground, a flood gate should be provided at the end section.

9.9.3.   When bodies of water or explosive gases may be encountered, trial boreholes should be drilled ahead of the workings.

9.9.4.   Reliable means of communication between workers inside pipes and persons outside should be provided.

9.9.5.   It should be possible for workers employed in piping to reach a safe place quickly in an emergency.

9.9.6.   Adequate arrangements should be made to rescue workers who are in danger and cannot reach a safe place.

10. Cofferdams and caissons and work in compressed air

10.1. General provisions

10.1.1. Every cofferdam and caisson should be:

(a) of good construction and suitable and sound material and of adequate strength;

(b) provided with adequate means for workers to reach safety in the event of an inrush of water or material;

(c) provided with safe means of access to every place where workers are employed.

10.1.2. The construction, positioning, modification or dismantling of a cofferdam or caisson should take place only under the immediate supervision of a competent person.

10.1.3. Every cofferdam and caisson should be inspected by a competent person at intervals prescribed by national laws or regulations.

10.1.4. A person should only be allowed to work in a cofferdam or caisson if it has been inspected and found safe by a competent person within such preceding period as is prescribed by national laws or regulations and the results thereof recorded in a prescribed form or register.

10.1.5. Work in compressed air should be carried out only in accordance with measures prescribed by national laws or regulations.

10.1.6. Work in compressed air should be carried out only by workers who are 18 years old or more and who have been medically examined and found fit for such employment.

10.1.7. Work in compressed air should be carried out only

when a competent person is present to supervise the conduct of operations.

10.1.8. National laws or regulations should lay down conditions in which the work is to be carried out and the plant and equipment are to be used and provide for health surveillance of workers and the duration of work in compressed air.

10.1.9. No person should be employed in compressed air unless he is under the constant supervision of an experienced person and properly instructed and supplied with a leaflet containing advice as to the precautions to be taken in connection with such work.

10.1.10. No person should be subjected to a pressure exceeding 2.5 bar except in emergencies.

10.1.11. For every shift a record should be kept showing the time every worker spends in the working chamber and the time taken for decompression.

10.1.12. If the air pressure exceeds 1 bar, the medical examination of the worker should have been carried out within the four weeks preceding his employment.

10.1.13. Workers who have been employed continuously in compressed air at a pressure less than 1 bar should be medically re-examined every two months; if the pressure is higher, the period between re-examinations should be shorter.

10.1.14. Workers who have been absent from work in compressed air for any period due to illness or for ten days or more for reasons other than illness should be medically re-examined. Such workers should be reintroduced into compressed-air work in a graduated manner.

10.1.15. For every project where workers are employed in compressed air, a physician or a nurse or a trained first-aid attendant familiar with compressed-air work should be available at all times.

10.1.16.   When persons are employed in compressed air at a pressure exceeding 1 bar the employer should inform a neighbouring hospital of the position of the worksite and of the name and address of the physician exercising medical supervision.

10.1.17.   Every person employed in compressed air at a pressure exceeding 1 bar should be provided with an identification badge to be worn on the body indicating that he has been employed in compressed air and giving the address of the medical lock at his place of employment.

10.1.18.   The identification badge should state that the wearer should be taken to the medical lock and not to a hospital if he is ill.

10.1.19.   Adequate and suitable facilities for remaining on the site after decompression, including shelters with seats should be provided for workers working in compressed air.

10.1.20.   Any person not previously employed in compressed air should not be subject to compressed air unless accompanied in the man lock by a person competent to advise him as to the appropriate conduct of persons during compression.

10.1.21.   During compression the pressure should not be raised to more than about 0.25 bar until the lock attendant has ascertained that no person is complaining of discomfort, and thereafter it should be raised at a rate not exceeding about 0.5 bar per minute.

10.1.22.   If during compression any person is suffering from discomfort, compression should stop and the pressure be gradually reduced.

10.2. Work in cofferdams and caissons

10.2.1. When necessary to prevent danger, caissons and shafts should:

(a) be adequately braced;

(b) be firmly secured in position.

10.2.2. Before being taken into use, shafts should undergo an appropriate hydrostatic test.

10.2.3. Every caisson and shaft containing flammable material should be provided with a water line, sufficient hose connections and sufficient hose or appropriate extinguishers.

10.2.4. Every caisson, shaft, working chamber, medical lock and man lock should have a minimum internal height of 1.8 m.

Working chambers

10.2.5. Every working chamber should be provided with a wet-bulb thermometer.

10.2.6. Work under pressure when the wet-bulb temperature exceeds 28 C should be restricted unless it is absolutely necessary.

10.2.7. While any person is in a working chamber, the door between the chamber and a man lock leading to a lower pressure should as far as practicable be kept open if the lock is not in use.

Medical locks

10.2.8. Where the pressure in a working chamber ordinarily exceeds 1 bar, a suitable medical lock conveniently situated should be provided solely for the treatment of workers employed in compressed air.

10.2.9. The medical lock should have two compartments so that it can be entered under pressure.

10.2.10. While any person is employed in compressed air a medical lock should be in the charge of a suitably qualified person.

Man locks

10.2.11. Every man lock should be of adequate internal dimensions and equipped with:

(a) pressure gauges that indicate to the man-lock attendant the pressure in the lock and in each working chamber to which it affords direct or indirect access and indicate to the persons in the lock the pressure in it;

(b) a clock or clocks so placed that the lock attendant and the persons in the lock can readily ascertain the time;

(c) efficient means of verbal communication between the lock attendant, the lock and the working chamber or chambers;

(d) means of enabling the persons in the lock to convey visible or other non-verbal signals to the lock attendant;

(e) efficient means enabling the lock attendant, from outside the lock, to reduce or cut off the supply of compressed air to the lock.

10.2.12. Persons in the lock should not be able to reduce the air pressure except:

(a) under the control of the lock attendant;

(b) in an emergency, by special means that should normally be kept sealed or locked.

10.2.13. In every man lock there should be a suitable notice indicating the precautions to be taken by persons during compression and decompression, and after decompression.

10.2.14. Every man lock should, while any person is in

it or in any working chamber to which it affords direct or in-direct access, be in the charge of an attendant who should:

(a) control compression and decompression in the lock;

(b) if the pressure exceeds 1 bar, keep a register showing:

 (i) the times at which each person enters and leaves the lock;

 (ii) the pressures at the times of entering and leaving;

 (iii) the times taken to decompress each person.

Air supply

10.2.15.   Compressed-air installations should be provided with air-supply plant capable of supplying any working chamber with sufficient fresh air at the pressure in the chamber, and not less than 1.0 m^3 per minute per person in the chamber.

10.2.16.   Pollution of the air supplied to the caisson from a compressor or any other source should be prevented.

10.2.17.   All air lines should be in duplicate and be equipped with non-return valves.

10.2.18.   There should be a sufficient reserve of air in compressor installations to allow a safe margin for breakdowns or repairs.

10.2.19.   There should be a stand-by or reserve compressor for emergencies.

10.2.20.   Two power units supplied from independent sources should be provided for each compressor.

Signalling

10.2.21.   Reliable means of communication such as bells, whistles or telephones should be maintained at all times between the working chamber and surface installations.

10.2.22. The code of signals should be conspicuously displayed in convenient positions at workplaces.

Lighting

10.2.23. All locks and working chambers should be provided with adequate electric lighting.

10.2.24. There should be two separate lighting installations supplied from independent sources of current.

10.3. Work in tunnels in compressed air

10.3.1. The bulkhead separating the working chamber from areas of lower pressure should be of sufficient strength to withstand safely the maximum pressure to which it will be subjected.

10.3.2. When necessary to prevent danger in the event of rapid flooding, the bulkhead should be sufficiently close to the face or shield to allow the workers to escape in an emergency.

10.3.3. Safety bulkheads should be provided within 60 m of the working face in all tunnels having a danger of inrush of water or material.

10.3.4. If the compressor is driven by electricity, stand-by compressor plant should be provided capable of maintaining at least 50 per cent of the air supply if the electrical power fails.

10.3.5. If the compressors are not driven by electricity, not more than half of them should be driven from the same source.

10.3.6. Each air line should be equipped with an adequate air receiver, a stop valve, a pressure-reducing valve, and a non-return valve close to the man locks.

10.3.7. The air supply should be provided by duplicate air lines between the air receiver and the working chamber.

10.3.8. An adjustable safety valve should be fitted on the outside of the bulkhead to a separate pipe leading from the working chamber through the bulkhead to the outside air.

10.3.9. Where practicable, in addition to a suitable man lock and a material lock, tunnels should have an emergency lock capable of holding an entire heading shift.

10.3.10. A suitable medical lock should be provided when work in compressed air is carried on in tunnels at pressures exceeding 1 bar.

10.3.11. In all tunnels 5 m or over in diameter or height a well-guarded overhead gangway should be provided from the working surface to the nearest airlock with an overhead clearance of at least 1.80 m.

10.3.12. Every tunnel should be provided with a water line extending into the working chamber to within 30 m of the working face, sufficient hose connections at suitable places, and sufficient hose.

10.3.13. When blasting work is being done in compressed air in tunnels:

(a) no worker other than the blaster and his assistants should be in a working chamber while boreholes are being loaded;

(b) no worker should re-enter a working chamber after a blast until the fumes have cleared.

11. Structural frames, formwork and concrete work

11.1. General provisions

11.1.1. The erection or dismantling of buildings, structures, civil engineering works, formwork, falsework and shoring should be carried out by trained workers only under the supervision of a competent person.

11.1.2. Adequate precautions should be taken to guard against danger to workers arising from any temporary state of weakness or instability of a structure.

11.1.3. Formwork, falsework and shoring should be so designed, constructed and maintained that it will safely support all loads that may be imposed on it.

11.1.4. Formwork should be so designed and erected that working platforms, means of access, bracing and means of handling and stabilising are easily fixed to the formwork structure.

11.2. Erection and dismantling of steel and prefabricated structures

11.2.1. As far as practicable the safety of workers employed on the erection and dismantling of steel and prefabricated structures should be ensured by appropriate means, such as provision and use of:

(a) ladders, gangways or fixed platforms;

(b) platforms, buckets, boatswain's chairs or other appropriate means suspended from lifting appliances;

(c) safety harnesses and lifelines, catch nets or catch platforms;

(*d*) power-operated mobile working platforms.

11.2.2. Steel and prefabricated structures should be so designed and made that they can be safely transported and erected, and if required by national laws and regulations each unit should be clearly marked with its own weight.

11.2.3. In addition to the need for the stability of the part when erected, when necessary to prevent danger the design should explicitly take into account:

(*a*) the conditions and methods of attachment in the operations of transport, storing and temporary support during erection or dismantling as applicable;

(*b*) methods for the provision of safeguards such as railings and working platforms, and, when necessary, for mounting them easily on the structural steel or prefabricated parts.

11.2.4. The hooks and other devices built in or provided on the structural steel or prefabricated parts that are required for lifting and transporting them should be so shaped, dimensioned and positioned as:

(*a*) to withstand with a sufficient margin the stresses to which they are subjected;

(*b*) not to set up stresses in the part that could cause failures, or stresses in the structure itself not provided for in the plans, and be designed to permit easy release from the lifting appliance. Lifting points for floor and staircase units should be located (recessed if necessary) so that they do not protrude above the surface;

(*c*) to avoid imbalance or distortion of the lifted load.

11.2.5. Prefabricated parts made of concrete should not be stripped or erected before the concrete has set and hardened sufficiently to the extent provided for in the plans, and before use should be examined for any sign of damage which may indicate weakness.

11.2.6. Storeplaces should be so constructed that:

(a) there is no risk of structural steel or prefabricated parts falling or overturning;

(b) storage conditions generally ensure stability and avoid damage having regard to the method of storage and atmospheric conditions;

(c) racks are set on firm ground and designed so that units cannot move accidentally.

11.2.7. While they are being stored, transported, raised or set down, structural steel or prefabricated parts should not be subjected to stresses prejudicial to their stability.

11.2.8. Every lifting appliance should:

(a) be suitable for the operations and not be capable of accidental disconnection;

(b) be approved by a competent person, or tested under a proof load 20 per cent heavier than the heaviest prefabricated part.

11.2.9. Lifting hooks should be of the self-closing type or of a safety type and should have the maximum permissible load marked on them.

11.2.10. Tongs, clamps and other appliances for lifting structural steel and prefabricated parts should:

(a) be of such shape and dimensions as to ensure a secure grip without damaging the part;

(b) be marked with the maximum permissible load in the most unfavourable lifting conditions.

11.2.11. Structural steel or prefabricated parts should be lifted by methods or appliances that prevent them from spinning accidentally.

11.2.12. When necessary to prevent danger, before they are raised from the ground, structural steel or prefabricated parts should be provided with safety devices such as railings and working platforms to prevent falls of persons.

11.2.13. While structural steel or prefabricated parts are being erected the workers should be provided with and use appliances for guiding them as they are being lifted and set down, so as to avoid crushing of hands and to facilitate the operations.

11.2.14. Before it is released from the lifting appliance a raised structural steel or prefabricated part should be so secured and wall units so propped that their stability cannot be imperilled, even by external agencies such as wind and passing loads, in accordance with national laws and regulations.

11.2.15. At workplaces adequate instruction should be given to the workers on the methods, arrangements and means required for the storage, transport, lifting and erection of structural steel or prefabricated parts, and before erection starts a meeting of all those responsible should be held to discuss and confirm the requirements for safe erection.

11.2.16. During transport, attachments such as slings and stirrups mounted on structural steel or prefabricated parts should be securely fastened to the parts.

11.2.17. Structural steel or prefabricated parts should be so transported that the conditions do not affect the stability of the parts or the means of transport result in jolting, vibration or stresses due to blows, or loads of material or persons.

11.2.18. When the method of erection does not permit the provision of other means of protection against falls of persons, the workplaces should be protected by guard-rails, and if appropriate by toe-boards.

11.2.19. When adverse weather conditions such as snow, ice and wind or reduced visibility entail risks of accidents the work should be carried on with particular care, or, if necessary, interrupted.

11.2.20. Structures should not be worked on during

violent storms or high winds, or when they are covered with ice or snow, or are slippery from other causes.

11.2.21.   If necessary to prevent danger, structural steel parts should be equipped with attachments for suspended scaffolds, lifelines or safety harnesses and other means of protection.

11.2.22.   The risks of falling, to which workers moving on high or sloping girders are exposed, should be limited by all means of adequate collective protection or, where this is impossible, by the use of a safety harness that is well secured to a sufficiently strong support.

11.2.23.   Structural steel parts that are to be erected at a great height should as far as practicable be assembled on the ground.

11.2.24.   When structural steel or prefabricated parts are being erected, a sufficiently extended area underneath the workplace should be barricaded or guarded.

11.2.25.   Steel trusses that are being erected should be adequately shored, braced or guyed until they are permanently secured in position.

11.2.26.   No load-bearing structural member should be dangerously weakened by cutting, holing or other means.

11.2.27.   Structural members should not be forced into place by the hoisting machine while any worker is in such a position that he could be injured by the operation.

11.2.28.   Open-web steel joists that are hoisted singly should be directly placed in position and secured against dislodgement.

11.3 Cast-in-situ concrete structures

11.3.1.   The construction of cast-in-situ, large span and multi-storey concrete structures should be based on plans that:

(a) include specifications of the steel, concrete and other material to be used, including technical methods for safe placing and handling;

(b) indicate clearly the position and arrangement of reinforcements in structural elements;

(c) provide, if appropriate, calculations of the load-bearing capacity of the structure.

11.3.2.   During the construction of cast-in-situ, large span and multi-storey concrete structures, a daily record should be kept of the progress of the work, including indications of all data which could affect the curing of the concrete.

11.3.3.   Precise procedures for all stages of erection should be prepared and a competent person appointed to co-ordinate the work and check procedures.

11.3.4.   During pouring, shuttering and its supports should be continuously watched for defects.

11.3.5.   Loads should not be dumped or placed on setting concrete.

11.4. Provision of temporary floors

11.4.1.   All tiers of open joists and girders on which workers are employed should be securely covered with close planking or any other effective covering until the permanent floor is installed.

11.4.2.   Parts of the protection should only be removed to the extent required for the continuation of the work.

11.4.3.   In halls and similar buildings without intermediate walls, columns or chimneys, close planking may be replaced by working platforms with adequate safeguards.

11.4.4.   In buildings or structures of skeleton steel

construction, permanent floor filling should as far as practicable be installed as the erection progresses.

11.5. Formwork

11.5.1.   All formwork should be properly designed.

11.5.2.   Clear and concise procedures to cover all stages of work should be prepared.

11.5.3.   A competent person should be appointed to co-ordinate the work and check that the procedures are being followed.

11.5.4.   No changes should be made without consulting the co-ordinator.

11.5.5.   All materials and scaffolding should be carefully examined and checked with the drawings before being taken into use.

11.5.6.   The foundations should be checked to see that the excavated ground conditions are as the original soil report suggested.

11.5.7.   Shuttering should be examined, erected and dismantled under the supervision of qualified and experienced persons and, as far as practicable, by workers familiar with the work.

11.5.8.   The necessary information for the erection of shuttering, including particulars of the spacing of stringers and props to stringers, should be provided for the workers in the form of sketches or scale drawings.

11.5.9.   Lumber and supports for shuttering (forms) should be adequate, having regard to the loads to be borne, spans, setting temperature and rate of pour. Where necessary to prevent danger, adequate shoring should be provided to support slabs and beams as a protection against superimposed loads.

11.5.10. All adjustable shoring should be locked in position when adjusted.

11.5.11. Shoring should be so arranged that when it is being removed sufficient props can be left in place to afford the support necessary to prevent danger.

11.5.12. Shoring should be adequately protected from damage from moving vehicles, swinging loads, etc.

11.5.13. Shoring should be left in place until the concrete has acquired sufficient strength to support safely not only its own weight but also any imposed loads. It should not be removed until authorisation has been given by a competent person.

11.5.14. Shoring should be adequately braced or tied together to prevent deformation or displacement.

11.5.15. To prevent danger from falling parts when shuttering is being taken down, the shuttering should as far as practicable be taken down whole, or else remaining parts should be supported.

11.5.16. Mechanical, hydraulic or pneumatic lifting appliances for handling forms should be provided with automatic holding devices to prevent danger if the power of the lifting mechanism fails.

11.5.17. Vacuum-lifting appliances should only be applied to smooth, clean surfaces.

11.5.18. Vacuum-lifting devices should be provided with an automatic cut-off to prevent loss of suction in the event of a power or equipment failure.

12. Pile-driving

12.1. General provisions

12.1.1. All pile-driving equipment should be of good design and construction taking into account as far as possible ergonomic principles, and be properly maintained.

12.1.2. Pile-driving should be carried out only under the supervision of a competent person.

12.1.3. Prior to piling, all underground services in the area should be located and rendered safe.

12.1.4. Pile-drivers should be firmly supported on heavy timber sills, concrete beds or other secure foundation.

12.1.5. If necessary to prevent danger, pile-drivers should be adequately guyed.

12.1.6. Precautions should be taken if it is necessary to erect pile-drivers in dangerous proximity to electrical conductors to ensure they are first made dead.

12.1.7. If two pile-drivers are erected at one place they should be separated by a distance at least equal to the longest leg.

12.1.8. When leads have to be inclined:

(a) they should be adequately counterbalanced;

(b) the tilting device should be secured against slipping.

12.1.9. The hoses of steam and air hammers should be securely lashed to the hammer so as to prevent them from whipping if a connection breaks.

12.1.10. Adequate precautions should be taken to prevent a pile-driver from overturning.

12.1.11. Adequate precautions should be taken, by providing stirrups or by other effective means, to prevent the rope from coming out of the top pulley or wheel.

12.1.12. Adequate precautions should be taken to prevent the hammer from missing the pile.

12.1.13. If necessary to prevent danger, long piles and heavy sheet piling should be secured against falling.

12.2. Inspection and maintenance of pile-driving equipment

12.2.1. Pile-driving equipment should not be taken into use until it has been inspected and found to be safe.

12.2.2. Pile-driving equipment in use should be inspected at suitable intervals.

12.2.3. Pile lines and pulley blocks should be inspected before the beginning of each shift.

12.3. Operation of pile-driving equipment

12.3.1. Only competent persons should operate pile-drivers.

12.3.2. Pile-driving operations should be governed by suitable signals.

12.3.3. Workers employed in the vicinity of pile-drivers should wear ear protection and safety helmets or hard hats.

12.3.4. As far as practicable, piles should be prepared at a distance at least equal to twice the length of the longest pile from the pile-driver.

12.3.5. When piles are driven at an inclination to the

vertical, if necessary to prevent danger, they should rest in a guide.

12.3.6.   When a pile-driver is not in use, the hammer should be blocked at the bottom of the leads.

12.4. Floating pile-drivers

12.4.1.   When pile-drivers are working over water, all relevant precautions for work over water should be taken in accordance with this code and in particular a suitable boat should be kept readily available at all times.

12.4.2.   All members of floating pile-driver crews should be trained to handle boats.

12.4.3.   Floating pile-drivers should be provided with a whistle, siren, horn or other effective signalling equipment.

12.4.4.   Floating pile-drivers should be provided with adequate fire-fighting equipment.

12.4.5.   The weight of machinery on a floating pile-driver should be evenly distributed so that the deck of the installation is horizontal.

12.4.6.   Steel pile-driver hulls should be divided into watertight compartments.

12.4.7.   Watertight compartments should be provided with siphons for the removal of water seepage.

12.4.8.   Deck hatches should have firmly fastened covers that fit flush with the deck.

12.4.9.   Sufficient sheaves should be provided on deck to enable the pile-driver to be safely manoeuvred in any direction and safely secured in position.

12.4.10.   Regular head counts should be taken of the pile-driving crew members.

12.5. Sheet piling

12.5.1. If necessary to prevent danger from wind or other sources, handlines should be used to control the load.

12.5.2. Where practicable, a "gate support system" made up from timber "H" frames should be considered. If the gates are over 2 m high they should not be used as a working platform unless fitted with guard-rails, toe-boards and ladder access.

12.5.3. Remote release shackles should be used where possible. The length of the operating rope should be less than the length of the pile and the rope should be secured around the pile to prevent snagging, or being caught in the wind and becoming inaccessible.

12.5.4. If piles are too heavy for a remote release shackle and work cannot be carried out safely from a ladder, a lifting cage should be provided to gain access for unscrewing the shackle.

12.5.5. Long sheet piles should be pitched with a pile spreader. When this is not possible, a pile-pitching cage should be used which should hang from the adjacent pile. The operatives should be provided with a safety harness to be attached to the adjacent pile.

12.5.6. Workers handling sheets should wear gloves.

12.5.7. While it is being weighted with stones, etc., sheet piling should be securely moored.

12.5.8. Adequate pumping facilities should be available at cofferdams to keep them clear of water.

13. Work over water

13.1. General provisions

13.1.1.   Where work is done over or in close proximity to water provision should be made for:

(a) preventing workers from falling into water;

(b) the rescue of workers in danger of drowning;

(c) safe and sufficient transport.

13.1.2.   National laws or regulations should lay down provisions for the safe performance of work over or in close proximity to water which should include, where appropriate, the provision and use of suitable and adequate:

(a) fencing, safety nets and safety harnesses;

(b) lifebuoys, life jackets and manned boats (motor-driven if necessary);

(c) protection against such hazards as reptiles and other animals.

13.1.3.   Gangways, pontoons, bridges, footbridges and other walkways or workplaces over water should:

(a) possess adequate strength and stability;

(b) be sufficiently wide to allow safe movement of workers;

(c) have level surfaces free from protruding knots, bark, nails, bolts and other tripping hazards;

(d) if necessary to prevent danger, be boarded over;

(e) if necessary to prevent danger, be adequately lit when natural lighting is insufficient;

(f) be provided at appropriate points with sufficient lifebuoys, lifelines and other life-saving equipment;

(g) where practicable and necessary to prevent danger, be provided with toe-boards, guard-rails, hand ropes or the like;

(h) be kept clear of tackle, tools and other obstructions;

(i) be strewn with sand, ashes or the like when made slippery by oil or snow;

(j) be secured to prevent dislodgement by rising water or high winds, especially in the case of decking boards on gangways and platforms erected above tidal waters;

(k) if necessary, be equipped with ladders which should be sound, of sufficient strength and length and be securely lashed to prevent slipping. Where vertical permanent ladders are provided in plant over water they should be fitted with safety hoops;

(l) where appropriate, possess adequate buoyancy.

13.1.4.   Floating structures should, if necessary to ensure protection, be provided with shelters.

13.1.5.   Floating operational equipment should be provided with sufficient and suitable rescue equipment such as lifelines, gaffs and ring buoys.

13.1.6.   Where used, rafts should:

(a) be strong enough to support safely the maximum loads that they will have to carry;

(b) be securely moored;

(c) have safe means of access.

13.1.7.   Iron decks should be studded or have some other type of non-slip surface.

13.1.8.   As far as practicable, all deck openings including those for buckets should be fenced.

13.1.9.   A safe walkway should be provided on all floating pipelines.

13.1.10.   No person should enter a hydraulic dredge gear room without first informing the leverman and without being accompanied by a second person.

13.1.11. Hoist lines, drag lines, buckets, cutter heads and bridles should be inspected daily.

13.1.12. Workers should be embarked and disembarked only at suitable and safe landing places.

13.1.13. Regular head counts should be taken of workers involved in such operations.

13.2. Boats

13.2.1. Boats used to transport workers by water should comply with requirements which should be laid down by the competent authority.

13.2.2. Boats used to transport workers should be manned by an adequate and experienced crew.

13.2.3. The maximum number of persons transported in a boat should not be greater than safety allows and this number should be displayed in a conspicuous place.

13.2.4. Suitable and adequate life-saving appliances should be provided on boats and be properly placed and maintained.

13.2.5. Tow-boats should have a device by which the tow-rope can be quickly released.

13.2.6. Power-driven boats should carry suitable fire extinguishers.

13.2.7. Row-boats should carry a spare set of oars.

13.2.8. Rescue boats should be properly constructed and of sufficient length and beam to afford reasonable stability. For work in tidal waters or fast flowing rivers a power-driven craft should be provided, with a fixed self-starting device on the motor. Engines on powered craft when not patrolling should be run several times a day to ensure full efficiency.

13.3. Rescue and emergency procedures

13.3.1. Persons who work over water should be provided with some form of buoyancy aid. Life-jackets should provide sufficient freedom of movement, have sufficient buoyancy to bring persons to the surface and keep them afloat face upwards, be easily secured to the body, be readily visible, not be prone to snagging under water and have, when necessary, clip-on self-igniting lights.

13.3.2. Operatives should not work alone on or above water.

13.3.3. Each worker should be trained in the procedure to be followed in the event of an emergency.

14. Demolition

14.1. General provisions

14.1.1.   When the demolition of any building or structure might present danger to workers or to the public:

(a) appropriate precautions, methods and procedures should be adopted, including those for the disposal of waste or residues, in accordance with national laws or regulations;

(b) the work should be planned and undertaken only under the supervision of a competent person.

14.1.2.   Before demolition operations begin:

(a) structural details and builders' drawings should be obtained wherever possible;

(b) wherever possible, details of the previous use should be obtained to identify any possible contamination and hazards from chemicals, flammables, etc.;

(c) an initial survey should be carried out to identify any structural problems and risks associated with flammable substances and substances hazardous to health. The survey should note the type of ground on which the structure is erected, the condition of the roof trusses, the type of framing used in framed structures and the load-bearing walls;

(d) premises such as hospitals, telephone exchanges and industrial premises containing equipment sensitive to vibration and dust and all premises sensitive to noise should be located;

(e) a method of demolition should be formulated after the survey and recorded in a method statement having taken all the various considerations into account and identifying the problems and their solutions;

(f) a building should be checked and it should be verified that it is vacant.

14.1.3. All electric, gas, water and steam service lines should be shut off and, as necessary, capped or otherwise controlled at or outside the construction site before work commences.

14.1.4. If it is necessary to maintain any electric power, water or other services during demolition operations, they should be adequately protected against damage.

14.1.5. As far as practicable, the danger zone round the building should be adequately fenced off and signposted. To protect the public a fence 2 m high should be erected enclosing the demolition operations and the access gates should be secured outside working hours.

14.1.6. Demolition operations should only be carried out by competent workers.

14.1.7. The fabric of buildings contaminated with substances hazardous to health should be decontaminated and where necessary appropriate protective clothing and suitable respiratory protective equipment should be provided and worn.

14.1.8. Where plant has contained flammable materials, special precautions should be taken to avoid fire and explosion.

14.1.9. The plant to be demolished should be isolated from all other plant that may contain flammable materials. Any residual flammable material in the plant should be rendered safe by, for example, cleaning, purging or the application of an inert atmosphere as appropriate.

14.1.10. Care should be taken not to demolish any parts which would destroy the stability of other parts.

14.1.11. Demolition activities should not be continued under climatic conditions such as high winds, which could cause the collapse of already weakened structures.

14.1.12.   When necessary to prevent danger, parts of structures should be adequately shored, braced or otherwise supported.

14.1.13.   Structures should not be left in a condition in which they could be brought down by wind pressure or vibration.

14.1.14.   Where necessary to keep down dust, buildings being demolished should be sprayed with water at suitable intervals.

14.1.15.   Foundation walls serving as retaining walls to support earth or adjoining structures should not be demolished until the adjoining structure has been underpinned or braced, and the earth removed or supported by sheet piling or sheathing.

14.1.16.   Where a deliberate controlled collapse technique is to be used, expert engineering advice should be obtained, and:

(a) it should only be used where the whole structure is to come down because it relies on the removal of key structural members to effect a total collapse;

(b) it should only be used on sites that are fairly level and where there is enough surrounding space for all operatives and equipment to be withdrawn to a safe distance.

14.1.17.   Buildings and structures which are not carrying their design loads may be pre-weakened prior to a deliberate collapse, but in such cases:

(a) the pre-weakening should be carefully planned so that, despite the removal of redundant members and the partial cutting of load-bearing members, the structure should have sufficient strength to resist wind loads or impact loads until such time as a deliberate collapse is achieved;

(b) the dead load should be reduced systematically by the removal of surplus material, machinery, cladding, walls and parts of floors before work begins on the structural frame.

14.1.18. Where explosives are used to demolish key members, the blast protection and safe distances should be agreed in advance. The work should only be undertaken by personnel experienced in the controlled application of explosives in accordance with national laws and regulations.

14.1.19. The shot-firers should establish the area at risk to enable the area to be appropriately cleared or evacuated, if necessary. Blast protection should be of a high standard but should not be considered as an alternative to defining the area likely to be affected.

14.1.20. When equipment such as power shovels and bull-dozers are used for demolition, due consideration should be given to the nature of the building or structure, its dimensions, as well as to the power of the equipment being used.

14.1.21. If a swinging weight is used for demolition, a safety zone having a width of at least one-and-a-half times the height of the building or structure should be maintained around the points of impact.

14.1.22. Swinging weights should be so controlled that they cannot swing against any structure other than the one being demolished.

14.1.23. If a clamshell bucket is used for demolition, a safety zone extending 8 m from the line of travel of the bucket should be maintained.

14.1.24. Where necessary during the demolition of build-ings or other structures, appropriate catch platforms capable of withstanding safely a live load of 6.0 kN/m^2 and at least 1.5 m wide should be provided along the outside of exterior walls so as to prevent danger from falling objects.

14.2. Demolition of walls

14.2.1.   Walls should be demolished storey by storey beginning at the roof and working downwards.

14.2.2.   Where necessary, unsupported walls should be prevented from falling by means such as shoring and ties.

14.3. Demolition of floors

14.3.1.   When necessary to prevent danger, workers demolishing floors should be provided with planking or walkways on which to stand or move.

14.3.2.   Openings through which material is dropped should be adequately fenced or barricaded to prevent danger.

14.3.3.   All work above each tier of floor beams should be completed before the safety of the tier supports is impaired.

14.4. Demolition of structural steelwork

14.4.1.   All practicable precautions should be taken to prevent danger from any sudden twist, spring or collapse of steelwork, ironwork or reinforced concrete when it is cut or released.

14.4.2.   Steel construction should be demolished tier by tier.

14.4.3.   Structural steel parts should be lowered and not dropped from a height.

14.5. Demolition of tall chimneys

14.5.1.   Tall chimneys should not be demolished by blasting or overturning unless a protected area of adequate dimensions can be established in which the chimney can fall safely.

14.5.2. Tall chimneys should only be demolished by competent persons under constant competent supervision.

14.5.3. Workers should not stand on top of the chimney wall.

14.5.4. Material thrown down should only be removed during breaks in the work or under controlled conditions.

14.6. Use and removal of asbestos and materials and articles containing asbestos

14.6.1. Use and removal of asbestos-containing materials and articles such as asbestos cement sheets or asbestos insulation present particular health problems as they often involve dismantling or breaking large quantities of friable materials. The work should be performed in accordance with the relevant provisions of the ILO code of practice on *Safety in the use of asbestos*, in particular the provisions of Chapter 18 on construction, demolition and alteration work.

15. Electricity

15.1. General provisions

15.1.1.   All electrical equipment and installations should be constructed, installed and maintained by a competent person, and so used as to guard against danger.

15.1.2.   Before construction is commenced and during the progress thereof, adequate steps should be taken to ascertain the presence of and to guard against danger to workers from any live electrical cable or apparatus which is under, over or on the site.

15.1.3.   The laying and maintenance of electrical cables and apparatus on construction sites should be governed by national laws and regulations.

15.1.4.   All parts of electrical installations should be of adequate size and characteristics for the power requirements and work they may be called upon to do and in particular they should:

(a) be of adequate mechanical strength to withstand working conditions in construction operations;

(b) not be liable to damage by water, dust or electrical, thermal or chemical action to which they may be subjected in construction operations.

15.1.5.   All parts of electrical installations should be so constructed, installed and maintained as to prevent danger of electric shock, fire and external explosion.

15.1.6.   The electrical distribution at each site should be via an isolator which cuts off current from all conductors, is readily accessible and can be locked in the "off" position but not locked in the "on" position.

15.1.7. The power supply to all electrical equipment should be provided with means of cutting off current from all conductors in an emergency.

15.1.8. All electrical appliances and outlets should be clearly marked to indicate their purpose and voltage.

15.1.9. When the layout of an installation cannot be clearly recognised, the circuits and appliances should be identified by labels or other effective means.

15.1.10. Circuits and appliances carrying different voltages in the same installation should be clearly distinguished by conspicuous means such as coloured markings.

15.1.11. Adequate precautions should be taken to prevent installations from receiving current at a higher voltage from other installations.

15.1.12. Where necessary to prevent danger, installations should be protected against lightning.

15.1.13. Lines for signalling and telecommunication systems should not be laid on the same supports as medium- and high-voltage lines.

15.1.14. Only flameproof equipment and conductors should be installed in explosive atmospheres or in storeplaces for explosives or flammable liquids.

15.1.15. A notice or notices should be kept exhibited at suitable places:

(a) prohibiting unauthorised persons from entering electrical equipment rooms or from handling or interfering with electrical apparatus;

(b) containing directions as to procedures in case of fire, rescue of persons in contact with live conductors and the restoration of persons suffering from electric shock;

(c) specifying the person to be notified in case of electrical accident or dangerous occurrence, and indicating how to communicate with him.

15.1.16.   Suitable warnings should be displayed at all places where contact with or proximity to electrical equipment can cause danger.

15.1.17.   Persons having to operate electrical equipment should be fully instructed as to any possible dangers of the equipment concerned.

15.2. Inspection and maintenance

15.2.1.   All electrical equipment should be inspected before it is taken into use to ensure that it is suitable for its proposed use.

15.2.2.   At the beginning of every shift, the person using the electrical equipment should make a careful external examination of the equipment and conductors, especially the flexible cables.

15.2.3.   Apart from some exceptional cases, work on or near live parts of electrical equipment should be forbidden.

15.2.4.   Before any work is begun on conductors or equipment that do not have to remain live:

(a) the current should be switched off by a responsible person;

(b) adequate precautions should be taken to prevent the current from being switched on again;

(c) the conductors or the equipment should be tested to ascertain that they are dead;

(d) the conductors and equipment should be earthed and short-circuited;

(e) neighbouring live parts should be adequately protected against accidental contact.

15.2.5. After work has been done on conductors and equipment, the current should only be switched on again on the orders of a competent person after the earthing and short-circuiting have been removed and the workplace reported safe.

15.2.6. Electricians should be supplied with sufficient adequate tools, and personal protective equipment such as rubber gloves, mats and blankets.

15.2.7. All conductors and equipment should be considered to be live unless there is certain proof of the contrary.

15.2.8. When work has to be done in dangerous proximity to live parts the current should be cut off. If for operational reasons this is not possible, the live parts should be fenced off or enclosed by qualified staff from the power station concerned.

15.3. Testing

15.3.1. Electrical installations should be inspected and tested and the results recorded in accordance with national laws or regulations.

15.3.2. Periodic testing of the efficiency of the earth leakage protective devices should be carried out.

15.3.3. Particular attention should be paid to the earthing of apparatus, the continuity of protective conductors, polarity and insulation resistance, protection against mechanical damage and condition of connections at points of entry.

16. Explosives

16.1. General provisions

16.1.1. Explosives should not be stored, transported, handled or used except:

(a) under conditions prescribed by national laws or regulations;

(b) by a competent person, who should take all necessary steps to ensure that workers and other persons are not exposed to risk of injury.

16.1.2. Before explosives are used for blasting on a site, an agreed system of work should be prepared and the responsibilities of persons involved detailed in writing.

16.1.3. Blasting caps, safety fuses, wiring and other blasting equipment should conform to specifications laid down in national laws or regulations.

16.1.4. Dynamite should not be removed from its original wrapper until it is being loaded into boreholes.

16.1.5. As far as practicable, blasting should be done off shift or during breaks in the work.

16.1.6. As far as practicable, blasting above ground should be done in daylight.

16.1.7. If blasting above ground has to be done during darkness, roadways and pathways should be adequately lit.

16.1.8. If blasting can endanger workers in another enterprise:

(a) blasting times should be agreed between the two enterprises;

(b) shots should not be fired until a warning has been given to the other enterprise and acknowledged by it.

16.1.9. Loaded boreholes should not be left unattended after the end of the shift.

16.1.10. At an appropriate time before the final blasting warning, workers in the area should be removed to a designated safe place.

16.1.11. An unmistakable, audible, final warning should be sounded one minute prior to the detonation of explosives; after completion, when the person in charge has established that safe conditions prevail, an "all clear" should be sounded.

16.1.12. To prevent persons entering any danger zone during blasting operations:

(a) look-outs should be posted around the area of operations;

(b) warning flags should be flown;

(c) conspicuous notices should be posted at points around the area of operations.

16.1.13. Before a borehole is loaded all workers not employed in the blasting operation should withdraw to a safe place.

16.1.14. Smoking and open flames should not be allowed in the loading area.

16.2. Transport, storage and handling

16.2.1. All explosives supplied to and issued from a magazine should be accounted for and recorded, and unused explosives should be returned to the same magazine on the completion of the operation for which they were drawn.

16.2.2. Detonators should be stored or transported separately from the explosives.

16.2.3. Workers storing, transporting or handling explosives or travelling on vehicles carrying explosives should not smoke or carry open lights.

16.2.4. Road and rail vehicles used to transport explosives should:

(a) be in good condition and running order;

(b) have a tight wooden or non-sparking metal floor;

(c) have sides and ends high enough to prevent the explosives from falling out;

(d) in the case of road vehicles, carry at least two suitable fire extinguishers;

(e) be plainly marked by a red flag, lettering or otherwise to indicate that they are carrying explosives.

16.2.5. Explosives and detonators should be transported separately from the magazine to the workplace in their original containers or in special closed containers of non-sparking metal.

16.2.6. Different types of explosives should not be transported in the same container.

16.2.7. Containers should be marked to show the type of explosive kept in them.

16.2.8. Explosives should be permanently stored only in magazines which should:

(a) be at a safe distance from occupied buildings or areas;

(b) be substantially constructed, bulletproof and fire-resistant;

(c) be clean, dry, well-ventilated, cool, and protected against frost;

(d) be kept securely locked.

16.2.9. Only flameproof electric lighting equipment should be allowed in explosives magazines.

16.2.10. Flammable substances or sparking metal objects should not be stored or used in explosives magazines.

16.2.11. In explosives magazines or in a restricted and clearly marked zone around them:

(a) smoking, matches, open lights or open flames should not be permitted;

(b) firearms should not be discharged;

(c) combustible debris such as grass, leaves or brushwood should not be allowed to accumulate.

16.2.12.   Explosives magazines should not be opened during or on the approach of an electrical storm.

16.2.13.   If quantities of explosives and detonators have to be provisionally stored outside the main magazine, special accommodation should be provided, such as a special room, a portable magazine or a suitable container.

16.2.14.   Overshoes should be kept at each store and worn by people who have to enter them.

16.2.15.   Only persons authorised to handle explosives should have the keys of magazines, storerooms or cases for explosives.

16.2.16.   Containers of explosives should not be opened with sparking tools, provided that metal slitters may be used to open cartons or similar containers.

16.2.17.   Explosives should be protected from impact.

16.2.18.   Explosives should not be carried in pockets or elsewhere on the person.

16.2.19.   As soon as the approach of an electrical storm is detected, all workers should be removed from the area where explosives are stored or are in use.

16.2.20.   No explosives should be left lying about without supervision.

16.3. Disposal of explosives

16.3.1. Explosives should not be destroyed except in conformity with the manufacturers' instructions.

16.3.2. No material used in the wrapping or packing of explosives should be burned in a stove, fireplace or other confined space.

16.3.3. No person should remain within 30 m of a fire in which wrapping or packing material is burned.

17. Health hazards, first aid and occupational health services

17.1. General provisions

17.1.1. For works which by their very nature expose workers to hazards arising from the use or presence of chemical, physical or biological agents and climatic conditions, appropriate preventive measures should be taken to avoid any danger to the safety and health of workers.

17.1.2. The preventive measures referred to in paragraph 17.1.1 should place emphasis on the need to eliminate or reduce the hazard at the source and in particular should require:

(a) the replacement of hazardous substances, equipment or processes with substances, equipment or processes less harmful or hazardous to workers' safety and health;

(b) the reduction of noise and vibration caused by equipment, machinery, installations and tools;

(c) control of the release of harmful agents or chemicals into the working environment;

(d) training in manual lifting;

(e) proper working postures when workers are required to work in fixed working positions or when they are carrying out repetitive work;

(f) appropriate protection against climatic conditions likely to jeopardise health;

(g) where the foregoing measures are inappropriate:
  (i) instituting work practices which will eliminate or minimise danger to safety and health;
  (ii) supplying and requiring the use of personal protective equipment and clothing.

17.1.3. The employer should make arrangements for the identification and assessment by competent persons of health hazards presented by the use of different operations, plant, machinery, equipment, substances and radiations at the construction site and take appropriate preventive or control measures against the identified health risks in conformity with the national laws and regulations.

17.2. Occupational health services

17.2.1. The employer should provide for the setting up of or access to an occupational health service consistent with the objectives and principles of the Occupational Health Services Convention, 1985 (No. 161) and Recommendation (No. 171).

17.2.2. All workers should be subject to health surveillance.

17.2.3. Monitoring and control of the working environment and planning of safety and health precautions should be performed as prescribed by national laws and regulations.

17.2.4. A multiplicity of health hazards are present in construction work and every effort should be made to promote awareness of this fact and of the need to safeguard health.

17.2.5. Whenever new products, equipment and working methods are introduced, special attention should be paid to informing and training workers with respect to the implications for safety and health.

17.3. First aid

17.3.1. The employer should be responsible for ensuring that first aid, including the provision of trained personnel, is available. Arrangements should be made for ensuring the removal for medical attention of workers who have suffered an accident or sudden illness.

17.3.2.   The manner in which first-aid facilities and personnel are to be provided should be prescribed by national laws or regulations, and drawn up after consulting the competent health authority and the most representative organisations of employers and workers concerned.

17.3.3.   Where the work involves risk of drowning, asphyxiation or electric shock, first-aid personnel should be proficient in the use of resuscitation and other life-saving techniques and in rescue procedures.

17.3.4.   Suitable rescue and resuscitation equipment, as required, including stretchers should be kept readily available at the construction site.

17.3.5.   First-aid kits or boxes, as appropriate, should be provided at the workplaces, including isolated locations such as maintenance gangs, and on motor vehicles, locomotives, boats and floating equipment, and be protected against contamination by dust, moisture, etc.

17.3.6.   First-aid kits and boxes should not contain anything besides material for first aid in emergencies.

17.3.7.   First-aid kits and boxes should contain simple and clear instructions to be followed, be kept under the charge of a responsible person qualified to render first aid and be regularly inspected and kept properly stocked.

17.3.8.   If a minimum number of workers as prescribed is employed in any shift, at least one suitably equipped first-aid room or station under the charge of qualified first-aid personnel or a nurse should be provided at a readily accessible place for treatment of minor injuries and as a rest place for seriously sick or injured workers.

17.4. Hazardous substances

17.4.1. An information system should be set up by the competent authority, using the results of international scientific research, to provide information for clients, architects, contractors, employers' and workers' representatives on the health risks associated with the hazardous substances used in the construction industry.

17.4.2. National laws and regulations should require that the manufacturers, importers and suppliers of hazardous products used in the construction industry should provide information with the products, in the appropriate language, on associated health risks and on the precautions to be taken.

17.4.3. In the use of materials that contain hazardous substances and in the removal and disposal of waste, the health of workers and of the public and the preservation of the environment should be safeguarded as prescribed by national laws and regulations.

17.4.4. Hazardous substances should be clearly labelled giving their relevant characteristics and instructions on their use. They should be handled under conditions prescribed by national laws and regulations or by the competent authority.

17.4.5. Containers of hazardous substances should carry or be accompanied by instructions for the safe handling of the contents and procedures to be followed in case of a spillage.

17.4.6. The competent authority, in consultation with the most representative organisations of employers and workers, should determine which hazardous substances should be prohibited from use in the construction industry.

17.4.7. Preference should be given to the application of hazardous substances by means other than spraying, such as by brush or roller, when feasible.

17.4.8.   Where the use of toxic solvents, certain thinners, certain paints or volatile chemical substances cannot be avoided, special precautions should be taken such as providing general and local exhaust ventilation, and, if this is not practicable or is inadequate, respiratory protective equipment should be used. Such measures should be applied more rigorously in situations when such chemicals are heated or used in confined spaces. Paints and adhesives which present health hazards should be replaced with water-dispersed products.

17.4.9.   Skin contact with hazardous chemicals should be avoided, particularly when dealing with chemicals which can penetrate through intact skin (e.g. certain wood preservatives) or can cause dermatitis (e.g. wet cement). Personal hygiene and the type of clothing worn should be such as to enable the rapid removal of any chemical from skin contact. Where allergic effects caused by certain materials could be reduced by introducing other additives, necessary steps should be taken to make use of these additives preferably at the manufacturing stage (e.g. adding iron sulphate to cement and cement products containing hexavalent chromium).

17.4.10.   When it is necessary to deal with proven carcinogenic substances, particularly in work involving bituminous or tar asphalt, asbestos fibres, pitch, some heavy oils, and some aromatic solvents, strict measures should be taken to avoid inhalation and skin contact. Particular care should be taken with substances where there is reliable evidence of suspected carcinogenic effects.

17.5. Dangerous atmospheres

17.5.1.   Where workers are required to enter any area in which a toxic or harmful substance may be present, or in which there may be an oxygen deficiency or a flammable atmosphere, adequate measures should be taken to guard against danger.

17.5.2.   The measures regarding dangerous atmospheres to be taken pursuant to paragraph 17.4.1 above should be prescribed by the competent authority and should include prior written authority or permission from a competent person, or any other system by which entry into any area in which a dangerous atmosphere may be present can be effected only after completing specified procedures.

17.5.3.   No naked light or flame or hot work such as welding, cutting and soldering should be permitted inside a confined space or area unless it has been made completely free of the flammable atmosphere, tested and found safe by a competent person. Only non-sparking tools and flameproof hand lamps protected with guard and safety torches should be used inside such confined space or area for initial inspection, cleaning or other work required to be done for making the area safe.

17.5.4.   No person should enter a confined space or area with a dangerous atmosphere or deficiency of oxygen unless:

(a) the atmosphere has been found to be safe after suitable testing by a competent person (which should be repeated at suitable intervals);

(b) adequate ventilation is provided.

17.5.5.   If the conditions in the preceding paragraph cannot conveniently be fulfilled, persons may enter such spaces for prescribed periods using air lines or self-contained breathing apparatus and safety harnesses with lifelines.

17.5.6.   While a worker is in a confined space:

(a) adequate facilities and equipment including breathing apparatus, resuscitation apparatus and oxygen should be readily available for rescue purposes;

(b) a fully trained attendant or attendants should be stationed at or near the opening;

(c) suitable means of communication should be maintained between the worker and the attendant or attendants.

17.6. Radiation hazards

Ionising radiations

17.6.1. Stringent safety regulations should be drawn up and enforced by the competent authority with respect to construction workers engaged in the construction, maintenance, renovation, demolition or dismantling of any buildings in which there is a risk of exposure to ionising radiations, in particular in the nuclear power industry, and in work using radioactive sources or inside structures containing natural radioactive materials.

17.6.2. Relevant provisions of the ILO code of practice on *Radiation protection of workers (Ionising radiations)* should be followed.

Non-ionising radiations

17.6.3. Workers performing operations where they are exposed to non-ionising radiations should be provided with adequate protection, and particularly in welding, torch cutting and soldering operations, with eye and face protection.

17.6.4. For the purpose of detecting pre-cancerous lesions of the skin, workers continually working under non-ionising radiation exposure, including exposure to the sun, should be under medical surveillance, where appropriate.

17.7. Heat stress, cold and wet conditions

17.7.1. Whenever heat stress, cold or wet conditions are such that they can lead to impairment of health or extreme discomfort, preventive measures should be taken, such as:

(*a*) proper design of the workload and workstation, with special regard to workers in cabins, and command or driving operations;

(b) training, to enable detection of early signs of disorders;

(c) supply of protective equipment;

(d) routine medical surveillance.

17.7.2. When working in hot conditions, preventive measures to avoid heat stress should include rest in cool areas and an adequate supply of drinking water.

17.8. Noise and vibration

17.8.1. Employers should provide protection for workers from the harmful effects of noise and vibration from machines and work processes, by measures including:

(a) replacing hazardous machines and processes by less hazardous ones;

(b) reducing the exposure of workers;

(c) providing personal hearing protection.

17.8.2. Employers should consider the following developments and improvements in machines and processes:

(a) pneumatic drills and jackhammers to be replaced by hydraulic and electro-pneumatic hammers;

(b) remote operation for vibrators, jackhammers and drills;

(c) acoustic enclosure and improved design for compressed air discharges, and the cutters, blades and exhausts of internal combustion engines as well as the engines themselves;

(d) better means of supporting or holding manually operated tools in order to reduce the effects of vibration or better vibration damping on vehicle controls and seats.

17.8.3. Employers should give priority to the reduction of the duration of workers' exposure to noise and vibration when operating:

(a) jackhammers, drills and compressors;

(b) high impact noise tools such as cartridge-operated guns;

(c) manually operated vibratory tools, especially those operated upwards or in a cold environment.

17.8.4. Employers should provide personal protective equipment where the harmful effects of noise and vibration will be experienced by workers; this should include:

(a) hearing protection in accordance with national laws and regulations, which can be worn with a safety helmet;

(b) in the case of vibration, suitable protective gloves.

17.9. Biological agents

17.9.1. In areas where biological agents pose a hazard, preventive measures should be taken which take account of the mode of transmission; in particular:

− the provision of sanitation and information for workers;

− action against vectors, such as rats and insects;

− chemical prophylaxis and immunisation;

− the availability of antidotes and suitable preventive and curative medicine, mainly in rural areas;

− the supply of protective clothing and other appropriate precautions.

17.10. Additional provisions

17.10.1. The manual lifting of weights which presents a safety and health risk to workers should be avoided by reducing the weight, by the use of mechanical devices or by other means.

17.10.2. Waste should not be destroyed or otherwise disposed of on a construction site in a manner which is liable to be injurious to health.

18. Personal protective equipment and protective clothing

18.1. General provisions

18.1.1. Where adequate protection against the risk of accident or injury to health, including exposure to adverse conditions, cannot be ensured by other means, suitable personal protective equipment and protective clothing, having regard to the type of work and risks, should be provided and maintained by the employer, without cost to the workers, as may be prescribed by national laws or regulations.

18.1.2. Personal protective equipment and protective clothing should comply with standards set by the competent authority, taking into account as far as possible ergonomic principles.

18.1.3. Employers should provide the workers with the appropriate means to enable them to use the individual protective equipment and should require and ensure its proper use.

18.1.4. A competent person having a full understanding of the nature of the hazard and the type, range and performance of the protection required should:

(a) select suitable items of personal protective equipment and protective clothing;

(b) arrange that they are properly stored, maintained, cleaned and, if necessary for health reasons, disinfected or sterilised at suitable intervals.

18.1.5. Workers should be required to make proper use of and to take good care of the personal protective equipment and protective clothing provided for their use.

18.1.6. Workers should be instructed in the use of personal protective equipment and protective clothing.

18.1.7. Workers working alone on construction sites in confined spaces, enclosed premises or in remote or inaccessible places should be provided with an appropriate alarm and the means of rapidly summoning assistance in an emergency.

18.2. Types

18.2.1. Where necessary, workers should be provided with and wear the following personal protective equipment and protective clothing:

(a) safety helmets or hard hats to protect the head from injury due to falling or flying objects, or due to striking against objects or structures;

(b) clear or coloured goggles, a screen, a face shield or other suitable device when likely to be exposed to eye or face injury from airborne dust or flying particles, dangerous substances, harmful heat, light or other radiation, and in particular during welding, flame cutting, rock drilling, concrete mixing or other hazardous work;

(c) protective gloves or gauntlets, appropriate barrier creams and suitable protective clothing to protect hands or the whole body as required when exposed to heat radiation or while handling hot, hazardous or other substances which might cause injury to the skin;

(d) footwear of an appropriate type when employed at places where there is the likelihood of exposure to adverse conditions or of injury from falling or crushing objects, hot or hazardous substances, sharp-edged tools or nails and slippery or ice-covered surfaces;

(e) respiratory protective equipment, suitable for the particular environment, when workers cannot be protected against airborne dust, fumes, vapours or gases by ventilation or other means;

(f) a suitable air line or self-contained breathing apparatus when employed in places likely to have an oxygen deficiency;

(g) respirators, overalls, head coverings, gloves, tight-fitting boiler suits, impermeable footwear and aprons appropriate to the risks of radioactive contamination in areas where unsealed radioactive sources are prepared or used;

(h) waterproof clothing and head coverings when working in adverse weather conditions;

(i) safety harnesses with independently secured lifelines where protection against falls cannot be provided by other appropriate means;

(j) life vests and life preservers where there is a danger of falling into water;

(k) distinguishing clothing or reflective devices or otherwise conspicuously visible material when there is regular exposure to danger from moving vehicles.

19. Welfare

19.1. General provisions

19.1.1. At or within reasonable access of every construction site an adequate supply of wholesome drinking water should be provided.

19.1.2. At or within reasonable access of every construction site, the following facilities should, depending on the number of workers and the duration of the work, be provided, kept clean and maintained:

(a) sanitary and washing facilities or showers;

(b) facilities for changing and for the storage and drying of clothing;

(c) accommodation for taking meals and for taking shelter during interruption of work due to adverse weather conditions.

19.1.3. Men and women workers should be provided with separate sanitary and washing facilities.

19.2. Drinking water

19.2.1. All drinking water should be from a source approved by the competent authority.

19.2.2. Where such water is not available, the competent authority should ensure that the necessary steps are taken to make any water to be used for drinking fit for human consumption.

19.2.3. Drinking water for common use should only be stored in closed containers from which the water should be dispensed through taps or cocks.

19.2.4.   If drinking water has to be transported to the worksite, the transport arrangements should be approved by the competent authority.

19.2.5.   The transport tanks, storage tanks and dispensing container should be designed, used, cleaned and disinfected at suitable intervals in a manner approved by the competent authority.

19.2.6.   Water that is unfit to drink should be conspicuously indicated by notices prohibiting workers from drinking it.

19.2.7.   A supply of drinking water should never be connected to a supply of water that is unfit to drink.

19.3. Sanitary facilities

19.3.1.   The scale of provision of toilet or sanitary facilities, and the construction and installation of water flush toilets, privies, chemical closets, plumbing or other toilet fixtures should comply with the requirements of the competent authority.

19.3.2.   No toilet other than a water flush toilet should be installed in any building containing sleeping, eating or other living accommodation and should be adequately ventilated and not open directly into occupied rooms.

19.3.3.   Adequate washing facilities should be provided as near as practicable to toilet facilities.

19.4. Washing facilities

19.4.1.   The number and standard of construction and maintenance of washing facilities should comply with the requirements of the competent authority.

19.4.2.   Washing facilities should not be used for any other purpose.

19.4.3.   Where workers are exposed to skin contamination by poisonous, infectious or irritating substances, or oil, grease or dust, there should be a sufficient number of appropriate washing facilities or shower-baths supplied with hot and cold water.

19.5. Cloakrooms

19.5.1.   Cloakrooms should be provided for workers at easily accessible places and not be used for any other purpose.

19.5.2.   Cloakrooms should be provided with suitable facilities for drying wet clothes and for hanging clothing including, where necessary to avoid contamination, suitable lockers separating working from street clothes.

19.5.3.   Suitable arrangements should be made for disinfecting cloakrooms and lockers in conformity with the requirements of the competent authority.

19.6. Facilities for food and drink

19.6.1.   In appropriate cases, depending on the number of workers, the duration of the work and its location, adequate facilities for obtaining or preparing food and drink at or near a construction site should be provided, if not otherwise available.

19.7. Shelters

19.7.1.   Shelters should, as far as practicable, provide facilities for washing, taking meals and for drying and storing clothing, unless such facilities are available in the vicinity.

19.8. Living accommodation

19.8.1.   Suitable living accommodation should be made available for the workers at construction sites which are remote from their homes, where adequate transportation between the site and their homes or other suitable living accommodation is not available. Men and women workers should be provided with separate sanitary, washing and sleeping facilities.

20. Information and training

20.1.   Workers should be adequately and suitably:

(a) informed of potential safety and health hazards to which they may be exposed at their workplace;

(b) instructed and trained in the measures available for the prevention and control, and protection against, those hazards.

20.2.   No person should be employed in any work at a construction site unless that person has received the necessary information, instruction and training so as to be able to do the work competently and safely. The competent authority should, in collaboration with employers, promote training programmes to enable all the workers to read and understand the information and instructions related to safety and health matters.

20.3.   The information, instruction and training should be given in a language understood by the worker and written, oral, visual and participative approaches should be used to ensure that the worker has assimilated the material.

20.4.   National laws or regulations should prescribe:

(a) the nature and length of training or retraining required for various categories of workers employed in construction projects;

(b) that the employer has the duty to set up appropriate training schemes or arrange to train or retrain various categories of workers.

20.5.   Every worker should receive instruction and training regarding the general safety and health measures common to the construction site, which should include:

(a) general rights and duties of workers at the construction site;

(b) means of access and egress both during normal working and in an emergency;

(c) measures for good housekeeping;

(d) location and proper use of welfare amenities and first-aid facilities provided in pursuance of the relevant provisions of this code;

(e) proper use and care of the items of personal protective equipment and protective clothing provided to the worker;

(f) general measures for personal hygiene and health protection;

(g) fire precautions to be taken;

(h) action to be taken in case of an emergency;

(i) requirements of relevant safety and health rules and regulations.

20.6. Copies of the relevant safety and health rules, regulations and procedures should be available to workers upon the commencement of and upon any change of employment.

20.7. Specialised instruction and training should be given to:

(a) drivers and operators of lifting appliances, transport vehicles, earth-moving and materials-handling equipment and plant, and machinery or equipment of a specialised or dangerous nature;

(b) workers engaged in the erection or dismantling of scaffolds;

(c) workers engaged in excavations deep enough to cause danger, or shafts, earthworks, underground works or tunnels;

(d) workers handling explosives or engaged in blasting operations;

(e) workers engaged in pile-driving;

(f) workers working in compressed air, cofferdams and caissons;

(g) workers engaged in the erection of prefabricated parts or steel structural frames and tall chimneys, and in concrete work, formwork and such other work;

(h) workers handling hazardous substances;

(i) workers working as signallers;

(j) other specialised categories of workers.

20.8.   Wherever required by national laws and regulations, only drivers, operators or attendants holding a certificate of proficiency or licence should be employed to operate particular vehicles, lifting appliances, boilers or other equipment.

21. Reporting of accidents and diseases

21.1.   National laws or regulations should provide for the reporting of occupational accidents and diseases to the competent authority.

21.2.   All accidents to workers causing loss of life or serious injury should be reported forthwith to the competent authority and an investigation of these accidents should be made.

21.3.   Other injuries causing incapacity for work for periods of time as may be specified in national laws or regulations, and prescribed occupational diseases should be reported to the competent authority within such time and in such form as may be specified.

21.4.   Dangerous occurrences such as:

(a) explosions and serious fires;

(b) the collapse of cranes, derricks or other lifting appliances;

(c) the collapse of buildings, structures or scaffolds, or parts thereof,

should be reported forthwith to the competent authority in such form and manner as may be prescribed, whether any personal injury has been caused or not.

Appendix

Bibliography

I. ILO publications

Listed below are various Conventions, Recommendations, codes of practice, guides and other ILO publications, which may assist the reader seeking further information about safety and health in construction.

Although this list is current as of the date of publication of this code of practice, the ILO is constantly publishing new material; for the most up-to-date information the reader is advised to contact:

- ILO Publications, International Labour Office, CH-1211 Geneva 22, Switzerland;
- International Occupational Safety and Health Information Centre (CIS), International Labour Office, Geneva, or any available CIS National Centre;
- any available ILO local or regional office.

Conventions

No. Title

81 Labour Inspection in Industry and Commerce, 1947

115 Protection of Workers against Ionising Radiations, 1960

119 Guarding of Machinery, 1963

121 Benefits in the Case of Employment Injury, 1964

127 Maximum Permissible Weight to Be Carried by One Worker, 1967

136 Protection against Hazards of Poisoning Arising from Benzene, 1971

138 Minimum Age for Admission to Employment, 1973

139 Prevention and Control of Occupational Hazards caused by Carcino-genic Substances and Agents, 1974

148 Protection of Workers against Occupational Hazards in the Working Environment Due to Air Pollution, Noise and Vibration, 1977

152 Occupational Safety and Health in Dock Work, 1979

155 Occupational Safety and Health and the Working Environment, 1981

160 Labour Statistics, 1985

161 Occupational Health Services, 1985

162 Safety in the Use of Asbestos, 1986

167 Safety and Health in Construction, 1988

170 Safety in the Use of Chemicals at Work, 1990

Recommendations

No. Title

81 Labour Inspection, 1947

97 Protection of the Health of Workers in Places of Employment, 1953

114 Protection of Workers against Ionising Radiations, 1960

118 Guarding of Machinery, 1963

121 Benefits in the Case of Employment Injury, 1964

128 Maximum Permissible Weight to Be Carried by One Worker, 1967

144 Protection against Hazards of Poisoning Arising from Benzene, 1971

146 Minimum Age for Admission to Employment, 1973

147 Prevention and Control of Occupational Hazards caused by Carcinogenic Substances and Agents, 1974

156 Protection of Workers against Occupational Hazards in the Working Environment Due to Air Pollution, Noise and Vibration, 1977

160 Occupational Safety and Health in Dock Work, 1979

164 Occupational Safety and Health and the Working Environment, 1981

170 Labour Statistics, 1985

171 Occupational Health Services, 1985

172 Safety in the Use of Asbestos, 1986

175 Safety and Health in Construction, 1988

177 Safety in the Use of Chemicals at Work, 1990

Codes of practice

Safe construction and installation of electric passenger, goods and service lifts. 1972. 108 pp.

Safety and health in building and civil engineering work.   1972.   386 pp.

Safety and health in shipbuilding and ship repairing.   1974.   260 pp.

Safety and health in dock work.   1977.   221 pp.

Safe design and use of chain saws.   1978.   71 pp.

Occupational exposure to airborne substances harmful to health.   1980.   44 pp.

Safety and health in the construction of fixed offshore installations in the petroleum industry.   1981.   135 pp.

Protection of workers against noise and vibration in the working environment.   1984.   90 pp.

Safety in the use of asbestos.   1984.   116 pp.

Radiation protection of workers (Ionising radiations).   1987.   71 pp.

Safety, health and working conditions in the transfer of technology to developing countries.   1988.   81 pp.

Prevention of major industrial accidents.   1991.   108 pp.

Guides and manuals

Manual of industrial radiation protection (six parts).   1963-68.

Guide to the prevention and suppression of dust in mining, tunnelling and quarrying.   1965.   421 pp.

Labour inspection, purposes and practice.   1973.   234 pp.

Working conditions and environment: A workers' education manual.   1983.   81 pp.

Accident prevention: A workers' education manual.   1986.   175 pp.

Safety, health and working conditions: Training manual. Joint Industrial Safety Council of Sweden/ILO.   1987.   106 pp.

Training manual on safety and health in construction.   1987.   347 pp.

Major hazard control: A practical manual.   1988.   296 pp.

Training manual on safety, health and welfare on construction sites.   1990.   210 pp.

Occupational Safety and Health Series

No. 22 Guidelines for the use of ILO international classification of radiographs of pneumoconioses.   Revised edition 1980.   48 pp.

No. 37 Occupational exposure limits for airborne toxic substances. 1981. 290 pp.

No. 38 Safe use of pesticides. 1977. 42 pp.

No. 39 Occupational cancer: Prevention and control. 1977. 36 pp.

No. 42 Building work: A compendium of occupational safety and health practice. 1979. 256 pp.

No. 43 Optimisation of the working environment: New trends. 1979. 421 pp.

No. 44 Ergonomic principles in the design of hand tools. 1980. 93 pp.

No. 45 Civil engineering work: A compendium of occupational safety practice. 1981. 153 pp.

No. 46 Prevention of occupational cancer: International Symposium. 1982. 658 pp.

No. 49 Dermatoses et professions. 1983. 95 pp. (French only).

No. 50. Human stress, work and job satisfaction: A critical approach. 1983. 72 pp.

No. 51 Stress in industry: Causes, effects and prevention. 1984. 70 pp.

No. 52 Success with occupational safety programmes. 1984. 148 pp.

No. 53 Occupational hazards from non-ionising electromagnetic radiation. 1985. 133 pp.

No. 54 The cost of occupational accidents and diseases. 1986. 142 pp.

No. 55 The provisions of the Basic Safety Standards for Radiation Protection relevant to the protection of workers against ionising radiations. 1985. 23 pp.

No. 56 Psychosocial factors at work: Recognition and control. 1986. 89 pp.

No. 57 Protection of workers against radio-frequency and microwave radiation: A technical review. 1986. 81 pp.

No. 58 Ergonomics in developing countries: An international symposium. 1987. 646 pp.

No. 59 Maximum weights in load lifting and carrying. 1988. 38 pp.

No. 60 Safety in the use of industrial robots. 1989. 69 pp.

No. 61 Working with visual display units. 1989. 57 pp.

No. 62 Guidelines for the radiation protection of workers in industry (Ionising radiation). 1989. 36 pp.

No. 63 The organisation of first aid in the workplace. 1989. 73 pp.

No. 64 Safety in the use of mineral and synthetic fibres. 1990. 94 pp.

No. 65 International data on anthropometry. 1990. 113 pp.

No. 66 International directory of occupational safety and health institutions. 1990. 272 pp.

No. 67 Occupational lung diseases: Prevention and control. 1991. 85 pp.

ILO Industrial committees and analogous meetings

The improvement of working conditions and of the working environment in the construction industry, Report II, Building, Civil Engineering and Public Works Committee, Tenth Session, Geneva, 1983.

Other ILO publications

Encyclopaedia of occupational health and safety. Third ed., 1983. 1176 pp. + 1361 pp.

Guidelines for the use of ILO international classification of radiographs of pneumoconioses. 1980. 48 pp.

Automation, work organisation and occupational stress. 1984. 188 pp.

Managing construction projects – A guide to processes and procedures. Edited by A. D. Austen and R. H. Neale. 1984. 158 pp.

Safety and health practices of multinational enterprises. 1984. 90 pp.

Introduction to working conditions and environment. Edited by J.-M. Clerc. 1985. 323 pp.

Register of lifting appliances and items of loose gear (Model form and certificates as required by ILO Convention No. 152). 1985. 16 pp.

Technology and employment in industry. Edited by A. S. Bhalla. 1985. 436 pp.

II. International Social Security Association (ISSA) publications

Various publications in different sectors of industry, including construction.

Information can be obtained from:

– ISSA Secretariat, CH-1211 Geneva 22, Switzerland;

– ISSA International Section for the Construction Industry: Secretariat, Organisme professionnel de prévention du bâtiment et des travaux publics (OPPBTP), Tour Amboise, 204, Rond-Point du Pont-de-Sèvres, F-925 16 Boulogne-Bilancourt, France.

Index